# HOW TO
# DESIGN A
# GARDEN

# HOW TO DESIGN A GARDEN

## JOHN BROOKES
MBE

PIMPERNEL
PRESS LTD
www.pimpernelpress.com

Edited by Gwendolyn van Paasschen

This book is dedicated to John Brookes MBE.

All royalties from *How to Design a Garden* will be donated to The John Brookes-Denmans Foundation.

Pimpernel Press Limited
www.pimpernelpress.com

*How to Design a Garden*
© Pimpernel Press Limited 2021
Text © John Brookes MBE and Gwendolyn van Paasschen 2021
Illustrations © The John Brookes-Denmans Foundation,
except for those listed otherwise on page 222.

A catalogue record for this book is available
from the British Library.

ISBN 978-1-910258-91-0

Typeset in Gill Sans
Printed and bound in China
by C&C Offset Printing Company Limited

9 8 7 6 5 4 3 2 1

FSC
www.fsc.org

MIX
Paper from
responsible sources
FSC® C008047

# CONTENTS

# PREFACE

'Just stop talking for a minute and look, the answers are all here.'

I remember John Brookes saying this to me in my early twenties; I had just graduated from university and little did I know at the time, but I was standing next to someone who would have the single greatest influence on my life of any man I would meet.

Brookes was of course right; he was determined to demystify what most designers had spent years clouding in the magic of being a garden designer. 'What is the point of designing something you can't justify?' he would say. And he was correct: for too long design was seen as a profession for those with a genius for creativity, and whilst Brookes had an unquestionable level of creativity, he also had a very rare talent for sharing it.

Standing in a garden with Brookes was rather like that wonderful moment when we first learnt to walk; we can't remember it happening, we all take it for granted, but we also know the complexity of thought which lies beneath. Brookes could read a garden in the same way others can master a landscape in oil paint; he would look beyond the requirements of the client, look through the interiors and out into the landscape beyond. It didn't matter if this landscape was a confusion of urban building or the rolling hills of Spain, Brookes understood the golden rule of contextualization to the local vernacular. This 'conversation', as he often called it, allowed for a refined decision making which can only lead to timeless gardens.

'Just stop talking for a minute and look, the answers are all here.' Brookes translated the language of the house architecture and generated a grid across the landscape. Often misunderstood as a basic introduction to design, the grid allowed an investigation on paper, the start of the design. Each as bespoke to the house as the eventual design. Terraces arose in perfect proportion, journeys through mass and void creating excitement and tension before allowing the eye to rest upon a well-placed tree or a sculpture. Planting, strong and structural, held the vision together like the stitches of the finest tailor. The finished garden met not only the client brief but also that of the site and its surroundings.

The greatest of John Brookes's legacy lies within the words of this book: 'A line is not simply a line; it is a conversation.'

Andrew Duff
30 March 2021

# FOREWORD

If John Brookes MBE had realized his dream of becoming a farmer somewhere in County Durham in the 1950s, the garden and landscape design professions would tragically have been very different. Garden design itself would have been very different, not just in Britain but also in many places around the globe.

I don't think that's too much of an exaggeration.

Fortunately, Percy Brookes could not afford to help his son procure a farm, but did help John get a three-year apprenticeship with the Nottingham Parks Department that taught him bedding out, management skills, even how to grow tomatoes and arrange cut flowers. The experience culminated in a six-month stint in the landscape architect's department where he learned the basics of design, draughtsmanship and 'the professional aspects of landscape design'. From there it was off to Baker Street in London to work for Brenda Colvin and Sylvia Crowe where he was immersed in the cutting edge of art, architecture and landscape design.

As the first independent designer to create an exhibition garden at the Chelsea Flower Show (1962), John's garden was also the first to showcase an outdoor living space rather than one where plants were laid out in a traditional style. Controversial though his design was, he won the Silver Flora medal. He was twenty-nine years old, and it was the first of seven exhibition gardens he designed at Chelsea (not to mention those he created as far afield as Russia and Japan). It was the beginning of a fifty-year career during which he overturned traditional notions of garden design in Britain and around the world.

John, a confirmed modernist, was the hot young designer in the 1960s, working on significant public and private projects, some for big names he would never drop. He even, apparently, earned a certificate in interior design from the Inchbald School of Design, for which he would open a school of interior design in Tehran in the late 1970s after being the Director of Garden Design Studies at the Inchbald School of Design.

Exposed to all kinds of thinking and the cutting edge of design during those early years – gardens are for people (Thomas Church), the garden could be an extension of the house (Brenda Colvin), gardens could be functional, low maintenance, more than a collection of plants, garden design is linked to art (Sir Geoffrey Jellicoe) – John was able to synthesize and balance creativity with pragmatism, style with reality, modernism with classicism, architecture with garden, design with the environment. He developed a philosophy combined with a technical approach to design that he taught, lectured and wrote about throughout his life. Along the way, his ideas and approach evolved, enriched by travel and imbued with the urgent need for conservation, sustainability and the overwhelming importance of preserving regional uniqueness.

This book is a collection of pieces he wrote during his long career that articulate his design philosophy and reveal the depth behind his thinking. Some are lectures, some are lessons, some are drafts of published articles, some are drafts of articles that were never published, and some seem to have been notes, perhaps to himself. He was known to wake up in the night and write about whatever was on his mind. Some pieces are dated, others are not, but they all remain relevant, prescient as they were.

The pieces reflect John's convictions, expressed in his own voice, aimed sometimes at his students, sometimes at colleagues, sometimes at homeowners; a voice that is at times querulous, humorous, cantankerous, patient, but always full of conviction. Ever thoughtful, John writes about the issues that concerned him most and occasionally those that concerned others more.

The purpose of this book is to remind these audiences of, and to introduce new ones to, the enduring relevance of John's design philosophy and the underlying thinking and issues that formed it and were catalysts in its evolution. The purpose is also, I hope, to provoke, to challenge, to inspire new discussions, debates and thinking.

Never one to dwell on the past, John would encourage us all to think about what the future of garden design should entail – to 'look', think, evaluate, argue, test, imagine, and continue to create with a sense of responsibility, especially with respect to the environment and the preservation of local identity.

Author, teacher, lecturer and designer, John won many awards in his lifetime, including the Award of Distinction from the American Association of Professional Landscape Designers (2004) and an honorary doctorate from the University of Essex (2006). He was made Honorary Fellow of the Kew Guild (2008) and received the Lifetime Achievement Award from the Society of Landscape Designers (2018). He was proudest of his MBE, awarded 'for services to horticulture in the UK and overseas' (2004), which he was deeply honoured to receive from Her Majesty, Queen Elizabeth, whom he had met when she had visited his Chelsea exhibition gardens.

Above all, John was one of the relatively few people whose vocation was also his avocation, and despite accolades, fame and awards he kept his feet steadfastly on the ground. He loved his students, he loved his clients, and he loved the challenges of each new site. As he said, 'I am the luckiest of men. I am a landscape designer.'

The lives of those of us who were lucky enough to know John were enhanced and altered in a uniquely significant and meaningful way. I knew John for twenty years, first as a mentor, then colleague and friend. He taught me to 'look', design, think, evaluate style, drive on the left side of the road and, unsuccessfully, to 'talk Geordie'. Compiling his writings here has continued my education, as I hope reading them will for others.

Gwendolyn van Paasschen,
Denmans, 22 January 2021

# PART I: LESS IS MORE

# ADVICE TO HOMEOWNERS

In his usual humorous, insightful and sometimes impatient way, John preached pragmatism and reality in the same breath as style and design. As a designer, he believed he could not please a client without achieving a balance. He followed the regime in working with a client that he recommends here to the homeowner: make lists of their needs and dislikes to help guide them; be practical; recognize the limitations of their budget, the amount of time and desire they have to work on their gardens; find a place to store mowers and bins, etc. John stipulates that the lifestyle of the homeowner as well as the architecture of the house and local vernacular should drive design decisions and, ever the modernist, advises that less is more. He reminds us that though there are many different elements one can include in the garden – from 'plastic-coated Gothic arches' to 'Victorian urns' – he advises against a piecemeal approach. He emphasizes building up 'a relationship of shapes which is what a garden's design is all about' and which is essential in creating a cohesive garden layout. From how to choose a pergola and place a pond, John provides a road map to creating a garden that suits the homeowner.

It is important to be sure you take the time to prepare your site thoroughly before both construction and planting.

# LESS IS MORE

I think it is vital to be practical in the development of your garden, and not get carried away in too many flights of fancy. Remember that the 30-metre/100-foot herbaceous border you saw one afternoon last June is maintained by knowledgeable staff, and you didn't see it either before or after that day! What I'm really saying is don't overreach yourself. It's impractical and even if you achieve your image, are you sure it is appropriate? Too much grandeur – and it's a gardener's dream to aspire upwards – too many urns or hard stone benches (or those dreadful white iron tables and chairs that leave an imprint on the bum) can look, not to mince words, pretentious.

So, don't overdo it, and when your desired effect isn't working don't add more bits. Take some away: 'less is more' was the modernist idiom and it still holds.

While maintenance capacity must dictate the extent to which you develop your garden, the style in which you do it will also. Formal layouts need much more time clipping and restraining the plants, since you are imposing an unnatural idiom upon your site. But even beyond this, it is a false economy not to prepare your site well, and to construct your layout properly. When you have the decks cleared is the time to really eradicate weeds or they will plague you forever more. Every region has persistent weeds that are difficult to stamp out after your garden is planted. So, really clear the deck.

It's well worth then spending a little more money at the outset on constructing your paths, terrace or steps properly, with the correct base and sub-base, because if you skimp on it, in a few years' time they will crack, wobble and be infested with weeds. They may well become dangerous too.

The time when you need to lay a terrace or build some steps, I know, is often the time when the kitty is at its lowest ebb. You've just bought the house, paid for its decoration, there are a mass of other bills to be paid, and the garden often comes last in the pecking order. In that case, just do a small part of the garden well for starters – seed the remainder to grass perhaps, or, if in the shade of trees, plant a ground cover than can later be replaced. Forms of lamium (dead nettle) cover the ground fast, as do ivy or periwinkle. The remaining parts of the layout can be completed in later years. This, incidentally, is the time to put your style ideas on plan and even have a design drawn up. It becomes the blueprint to which you can work over a period of time.

## THINGS TO CONSIDER
Before getting anything on paper, though – and this way you can get a firm estimate for any work proposed – you have to resolve what you want, and how much you will be able to look after without it getting on top of you. The sorts of thing which you must bear in mind, too, are that if you have a sit-on mower,

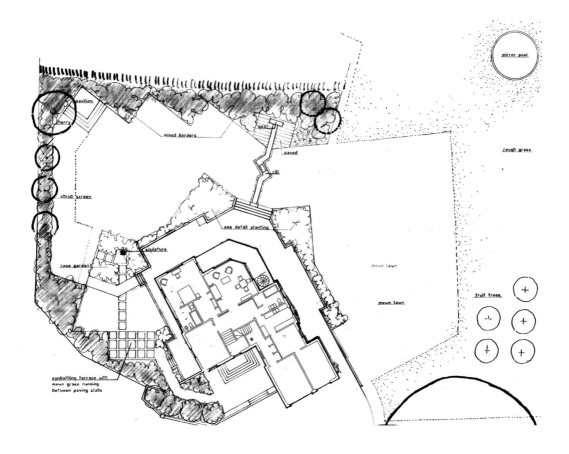

for instance, it doesn't like right-angled corners, and the compost heap should be close by in which to empty any cuttings.

A key to the sort of garden you will enjoy having, after assessing the site potential, is, of course, your house. From it you can take a proportion which will help with your layout later. The period or date of a house might suggest a small piece of history in the layout, and there is even a place for a certain amount of period restoration, although true restoration has to be done well with attention paid to every detail. For most people an essence of period is enough – a small herbal knot of santolina, hyssop, lavender or box, perhaps, for an original Tudor or even a modern Tudorbethan home.

The style of your house will give you a clue to the right style for your garden, as will the materials used in its construction. Most people do not live in a period home. We live in boxes made of brick or stone, or perhaps pebble-dashed or rendered. These are the clues to paving, curbs and garden buildings, for I would try to use some of the same house materials in the path or in the terrace, mixed with more modern slabs if brick is too expensive. You could

Once you have decided what kind of garden suits your house, site and lifestyle, draw up a plan. You can then develop the garden in phases according to your budget.

The materials of which your house is built will give you a
clue to the materials you should use in your garden.

include just one or two of these to blend with other materials to achieve some integration of the building into it.

Ultimately you can style your pots, seats and even plantings to a particular period when your house was built. For instance, ferneries were popular at the end of the 1800s and are excellent for a northern aspect. Some plants might have been popular as a reminder of a foreign posting. The moist warm conservatory evoked time spent in Burma or India perhaps, and pampas grass a reminder of the Argentine. Monkey puzzles were introduced at this time from Chile, then conifers from British Columbia and rhododendrons from the Himalaya. I do not think that one has to be rigid in plant selection according to date; it's just an interesting sidelight on plants and their popularity.

## A PLACE FOR EVERYTHING

When you have assessed your site, thought about the house and of what it is built, now consult yourself: the customer as it were. If your garden is to be practical it should work for you.

I think that a list is probably the easiest way to resolve this problem, particularly when more than one member of the family is involved. Perhaps

Take into account how much time you have to take care of a garden, how much space you have, and how to conceal rubbish bins and garden tools, especially if you have a small plot.

| REQUIRED | NOT REQUIRED |
|---|---|
| • a place for dustbins near the kitchen door, but covered so they won't smell | • no rockery unless you have natural outcrops (so much trouble with weeds for four weeks of colour) |
| • a place to hang some things to dry, despite the fact that you have a dryer | • no long grass – too untidy in a small garden |
| • a place for a few herbs: some chives, mint, parsley, basil and French sorrel | • no lawn – no place to store a mower and not enough sun |
| • a convenient tap for watering | • no water if it's a hazard for children |
| • a place to store logs if you have a fireplace | • no vegetables – the supermarket does a good job |
| • a place to make compost | • no flower beds – not enough time to take care of fussy plantings |
| • a place for oil tanks where applicable | • no messy trees that drop large leaves or fruits that need to be cleaned up |
| • a place for storing furniture, barbecue gear, children's play equipment – bicycles if the garage isn't big enough | • no shrubs that need annual shearing or pruning |
| • a terrace to eat on | |
| • grass to play on or a play space | |
| • a place for some wild flowers | |
| • a pond or a swimming pool | |

divide a page in two with, on one side, what you want to see out there and, on the other, what you don't want.

Perhaps include a third list with queries: who is going to look after the garden? And how much time will they have available for it? If the answer is that it is you who has to do the work, are you sure that you like gardening? I think it is perfectly valid to have a house with some land and recognize that, when you really get down to it, because of other commitments you are pressed for maintenance time. This is the crunch, for the less time you have the more necessary it is to have a strong simple basic layout with a minimum of frills. On top of this it is helpful to have a philosophy about your garden which does not constantly punish you if it is not immaculate. To hell with the neighbours, sort of thing!

EASY-MAINTENANCE GARDENS
For an easy-maintenance garden you need a sound layout which works for you: paths well laid in the right place, storage to hand with compost and rubbish bins easy to get at. Then ask yourself whether you need a lawn; must you grow vegetables and/or soft fruit? A pond can be tricky – the smaller it is, the harder to maintain. All hedges which need clipping can be omitted, and as much bare soil as possible should be covered. Roses, as much as you may want them,

need constant maintenance (with the possible exception of shrub roses), and perennials may need staking and/or dividing. So, what are you left with?

After getting your placement of features correct, think surfaces. You can bring visual interest into your site by mixing their textures: brick with stone, cobble with concrete slab, gravel with granite sett and so on. Try to incorporate a small change of level, too, which can make a feature.

Your planting needs to be massed and simple, with shrubs (some evergreen) and the occasional tree, depending on the scale of your garden. With perennials use strong architectural forms for interest against a shrub background that might include evergreen and variegated material. Remember that shrubs and trees flower as well as perennials, quite often with the added bonus of berries and autumn colour. You can also add colour with some spring bulbs in tubs or pots with summer annuals.

There is a whole range of biennial material that is very useful for an easy-maintenance garden. It includes things like foxgloves, nicotiana, evening primrose and verbascum, if you have alkaline soil, which will pop up each year

Mixing paving textures is a good way to add visual interest.

Strong architectural forms like this boxwood ball give structure to the garden all year. Architectural plants don't have to be clipped. They can have interesting forms that stand out, like yuccas or mahonias.

on their own where they self-seeded from the previous year. It is their random appearance combined with a shrubby fullness and strong layout that make for a good garden needing little attention.

Much of this reasoning is applicable to gardens for older people as well, or ones who just like to take it easy!

Raised beds to cut out bending or kneeling make good sense. Raise an area no more than 2 m/7 ft wide so that you can reach across, using brick, stone, railway sleepers, even slabs on edge, so that the soil is approximately 50 cm/18 inches high. Roses will be at a good height for spraying, deadheading and pruning, but include herbs with them to disguise their legginess. I think herbs are terrific value for all manner of uses as well as being fragrant and decorative in both flower and foliage. Many like lavender, rosemary, hyssop and savoury are evergreen as well in some climates. You can, of course, have a raised herbaceous planting dripping with lamb's ear or catmint on the outside, or a scree bed of shingle for alpines.

The raised container may have water in it, though this needs more careful detailing so children can't fall in it. A garden of raised beds will probably be formal in its layout and would look good in association with either paving or gravel.

## RENOVATING AN EXISTING GARDEN

There is another whole range of queries regarding a garden which is not new and which is established, even neglected. What to leave and what to take out? What can be cut back hard and when should it be done? You might have old trees that need attention – when you should call a tree surgeon for advice – but it will all be in the context of what you ultimately want the look to be.

Boundaries in older properties often present a problem, where not necessarily the whole fence should come down, just the rotting verticals be replaced. Old greenhouse structures are often a problem too. If you don't want it, and it is sound, try to sell it, using the old base perhaps as the basis for a terrace. Don't keep it, trying to fit a whole garden plan around it, when it's actually an eyesore.

Also into the eyesore category come other people's ideas of a trellis; quite often a good bonfire (provided you can burn) will soon settle that. If fires are out, you may have to pay someone to take away what it is you don't want.

The older the garden, often the more radical the changes needed, when old trees are casting too much shade, using up too much space, or impoverishing the ground around them. Check with the local planning office whether large trees have a protection order. If you live in a conservation area, check what you are allowed to do.

My advice on many of these factors is to not rush into a solution; live with your new site to really get the feel of what is necessary in both summer and winter, taking advice along the way, before doing anything which you might later regret. Remember that a predecessor often put something there for a reason. The reason might have now gone, the result may have got too big – but think before removing it!

Your garden's setting may provide you with clues about the right planting style.

## LAYOUT AND STYLE

It helps when evolving a garden's layout to have a basic survey drawn to scale. On that plan or on an overlay you put a site assessment of views, good and bad, sun, wind, etc. You can make yet another overlay taking those elements you want in the garden (having worked out with everyone what is wanted) and siting them in the most appropriate place. Each site will be different according to your permutation of what you want and what you've got. You can see how, when all these facets come together in the garden's layout, it begins to resolve itself. You should draw your overlay on pieces of tracing paper (readily available from an art store).

When you have finally made your placement decisions, this layout can now be interpreted in any number of different styles. Perhaps the location of your property may give the first clue to the style for you. Woodland, for instance, straight away brings to mind light shade, but is it birch spinney or trees with bluebells in spring followed by clouds of martagon lilies, or cool oaks with graceful ferns beneath in summer? Coniferous woodland is more difficult, for when conifers are young little grows in their dense shade. Only with age and height can they be trimmed up to allow light to penetrate downwards to a woodland sward. Each will have a different feel to it, made up of the types of path and planting on either side. Perhaps you go back to square one and restore the type of woodland that was originally there?

Then coastland – either sand dune, where little but dune grass will grow, or wind-blasted clifftops. A wider range of material than appreciated can stand a coastal location. For the first line of defence use pines with evergreen oak (*Quercus ilex*), then plant whitebeam, sycamore and thorn with escallonia, euonymus, hebe, buckthorn, elder and gorse beneath. Only when you have broken up the wind can you start to 'pretty up' with buddleia, cistus, daisy bush, fuchsia, pittosporum and hydrangea. Both will be dry gardens as well as windblown ones. They will be of their landscape, since nothing imposed or too decorative will survive these exacting conditions.

Apply the same sort of thinking to alpine or scree gardens, for some plants naturally thrive in shaded north-facing places with oozing water while others prefer the hot, sunny face. The plants of gravelly scree need excellent drainage in either sun or shade. Each location dictates what will grow where. This is a specialist field not lightly undertaken, best cultivated on natural outcrops of rock. The man-made rockery – a 1930s hangover – seldom looks satisfactory on the scale to which we now aspire.

Natural boggy areas can be exploited to become pools of water, making an ideal wildlife sanctuary. Plant flag iris, reeds, rushes or other natives for wildlife, with early yellow flowering marsh marigolds.

Ensure, however, that the water remains all year, flag iris being one of the few acceptable plants that can stand being both wet and dry at different times of the year. Remember that water plants are invasive: small pools disappear under their vegetation all too soon. Water plants generally prefer sunlight. Where the pool is in the shade of trees, leaf drop in autumn can foul the

water if its capacity is too small, but more than this, the charm of water is the reflection of sunlight upon it.

Any of these styles may be part and/or parcel of the next category, which to a degree has to do with the style of house which the garden surrounds.

A cottage garden of mixed muddle with gnarled apple trees, wormwood, rosemary, thyme and nasturtiums, with holly, hawthorn and hollyhock, bellflowers and pinks, sweet William and sweet pea – all simple flowers – may well surround a villa, but the imagery is more of an idealized thatched cottage than the subsistence gardens which they really were. Cottage gardens differed depending on where they were located – the range of available plant material getting more limited the harsher the climate. But the more obvious difference would have been the materials with which both the cottage itself as well as its surrounding garden were built.

The country house had much wider directional paths, which usually ended in a feature. Borders on either side of such a path would have been graded

A looser planting style suits less formal houses in more rural locations. Your garden should reflect the style of your house, both inside and out.

with strong colours in the foreground and getting paler as the border ran into the distance.

What is often not realized in a recent headlong rush to create traditional perennial borders is that they were not intended to last longer than six weeks or two months at the most, while a family was at its summer home. Even in their prime, these borders were constantly supplemented with pot-grown lilies, foxgloves and the like by an army of gardeners to maintain their floweriness.

After two world wars and a subsequent lack of cheap labour, these perennial borders had shrubby material added to them to cut down on their maintenance, when they became known as mixed borders. Now shrub roses, herbs and even grasses are included with perennials, lengthening their season of interest as well as adding texture.

In towns, smaller terrace gardens grew similar flowers, with often a small vegetable patch at the farthest point from the house. Tile work was typically introduced into paving with a rope-type curb or bricks used on edge to create a zig-zag line.

In the 1960s, as a town house movement gathered momentum there was talk of outside rooms with barbeques and play space for children. The 'designed' garden became popular with the heavy use of hard surfacing materials offset by architectural plants such as yucca and New Zealand flax.

Herbs began to be discussed as well, as we considered our diet more, and their merits as good garden plants. But in what form should the herbs be grown – a formal shape or just loose among perennials – and where should they be grown? I would suggest in full sun and near the house for easy picking. Actually, chives and mints can grow in shade too. Mint will grow and grow anywhere. Apart from their usefulness in the kitchen, herbs are wonderful just to brush against and pick the odd sprig as you walk down the garden.

There are other styles which are in the idiom of other countries. As travel became easier, more people have seen other styles and sought to recreate them at home. The Mediterranean look – be it Spanish, Italian or Provençal – is popular where the garden is hot and sunny and the owner likes to sunbathe. Culinary herbs with lavender, rosemary and cistus really come into their own here. There are small corners of paving and wisteria- and vine-covered pergolas, trickling water and decorative terracotta pots dripping with geraniums.

The Mediterranean look may surround a swimming pool, using flowers of clear blue, yellow or lemon. This is a tricky area to style – particularly if the pool is a demanding and virulent blue. Stick with brightness, for it's an area for action.

## COLOUR AND DECORATION

Colour, whether of foliage or flower, interestingly sets the mood of a garden quite often. So does location, according to the colour of the local soil, gravel, stone or brick, and whether it's a sunny garden in the morning or the evening, or whether it's a shade garden. For myself morning colours are bright and clear; evening colours are softer and more mellow. Colours for shade are white and limey green. But these are my personal preferences – my purpose is to suggest you make your own choices.

Another of my personal preferences is for rambling gardens – it's probably because I think they are easier to manage! But for many people rambling gardens look messy, and they like everything in neat rows, with clipped hedges and straight paths. For them, the precise geometry of a northern French garden, with its box hedges, clipped pyramids and axial views, might provide inspiration. It has to be said that this type of garden is far easier to lay out if you have the time to look after it. It's the school of gardening, too, that has a 'thing' at the end of each vista; it has arches and tunnels, mirrors with perspective tricks played with the widths of pathways. (You can seem to extend a garden's length by forcing its perspective: that is, a path which is 2 m/7 ft wide near the house is narrowed to 1 metre/39 inches at the far end. Visually it happens anyway – but you push it.) While these gimmicks are amusing if you visit a

garden, I would find them irritating to live with. And a passing bird all too soon reveals the mirror trick.

Having been so rude about mirrors, one of the most memorable Chelsea Flower Show gardens was of a supposed basement area, which was walled with angled mirrors with statuary in front. It was pure stage design in the images it created – not real gardening though.

Another popular natural style is that of Japan, although most of the gardens seen elsewhere under that guise bear little relationship to the original. What is wanted is an interpretation. In such a garden there will be little flower colour as plants are used for their form and shape – the spreading Japanese maples, bamboos of many forms, *Nandina domestica*, *Pinus mugo* – indeed pines of all types – with azaleas clipped into mounds. Rocks and boulders feature heavily with gravel and water; use flag iris too with shoals of sluggish golden carp. (Perhaps the figures of storks as heron frighteners really work!)

There are all sorts of Indian and Persian motifs which can be used in the garden. Such gardens are always formal, with tanks of water as central features and gentle fountains playing down their length. Pots of geraniums may be placed round the water feature in a symmetrical layout. A palm or citrus tree in a tub would help create the mood – though neither is reliably hardy unless in the most sheltered town garden. In temperate climates the hardy palm, *Trachycarpus fortunei* (the Chusan palm), or cordylines, particularly with age, might do the trick.

Persian gardens are associated with roses, and the deep yellow of all our roses comes from their *Rosa foetida* 'Persiana' – a double yellow 'old rose'. Such styles and plants would suit an enclosed town garden where the sound of trickling water might echo off walls rendered in exotic colours. With a clever use of tiles, such a garden can merge with an equally exotic interior decor.

## CONCEPT

Rambling gardens are easier to manage and if planted cleverly can provide colour all year. This planting of poppies and columbines starts the year with primroses and spring bulbs, then yields to later flowering plants like dahlias and roses. Grasses and sedum come on later and carry the look through winter.

The styles which I have described are readily recognizable where all the elements reinforce a basic concept. What happens more often is that a basic concept gets diluted with incorrect plantings, or colours, or periods or materials. Picture the typical brick home, built perhaps in the early 1970s: a square box with a sliding patio door. The garden at its rear has a cracked concrete terrace, with a 1980s conservatory over part of it. A willow from the neighbour's garden shades the bottom half of the plot, though where in sunlight a cottage garden is being attempted in beds that are too narrow, since lawn was necessary when the teenager was small. To enhance some low walls – dividing the cottage garden from the 'wild' garden beyond – are two Victorian urns picked up at a local sale, and between them a plastic-coated Gothic arch seen at the local flower show.

In the 'wild' garden is a stagnant pool, its water held by an all too apparent plastic sheet, as the water level has sunk since the dog will drink it. It's alive with frogs and other wildlife, however, so it's environmentally correct if not visually attractive. Somewhere in this mess sits a half-completed compost heap, started in the aftermath of a DIY gardening programme. All too familiar? Each idea at the time seemed wonderful but it's a piecemeal development which lacks a cohesive style.

The particular types of garden that I have described should get the thought processes moving to help you develop an overall look. To be more down to earth, however, most people's aspiration seems to be for specific features rather than a whole look, and perhaps it is easier to build up the style from that point.

## FEATURES

Let's start with a pergola. If I paint a picture of dappled light filtering through the leaves of a climbing rose hung with scented flowers, of the evening fragrance of honeysuckle and bunches of grapes temptingly beyond reach – you can see the attraction; throw in a perfumed wisteria and an early *Clematis armanii* and you have a winner.

But they are tricky things, pergolas, so go carefully. Decide first whether you want a colonnade effect, from which the pergola originated, or a pergola-covered room; then whether it will be free-standing or running off the house or a wall.

Free-standing pergolas can be bought but they tend to look 'thin'. Remember that they also divide up a space even more than the path they cover for they reinforce it, so you are left with a pit on either side. We tend also to make our pergola walks too narrow – particularly where you seek plenty of climbers to grow over them.

Pergolas over a terrace under which you might sit need to be large enough to span at least 3–4 m/10–13 ft. So you need thicker dimensions of wood, and hence bolder verticals, to support them. The ratio between width and height is quite tricky, if the end product is to look correct, particularly when the pergola runs off the house. If you can get the dimensions right, however, a pergola makes a lovely transition from in to out and can often improve the facade of a house. I think this is particularly so where a sliding or glass door, which is often bland, has been introduced later into a wall and provides too abrupt a transition. The pergola can soften that, and will not reduce light into the room if you get the spacing of the horizontals correct. How you style the pergola is a further consideration. It can be a brick support and painted beams, or wooden supports with similar beams. You can use metal verticals, stone columns, bamboo horizontals. There are a number of permutations.

'We want a pond' is often another primary desire, and before going further, a word of warning. Don't forget that a child can drown in as little as 2.5 cm/ 1 inch of water. When well planted and managed, a pool can be a joy. Incidentally, the larger it is, the easier it is to establish the necessary flora and fauna to keep the water clear.

So where to put this visually demanding thing – for it always becomes an eye-catcher? Near a terrace is nice, since water attracts all manner of birds, insects and small mammals to drink throughout the year. Such a placement

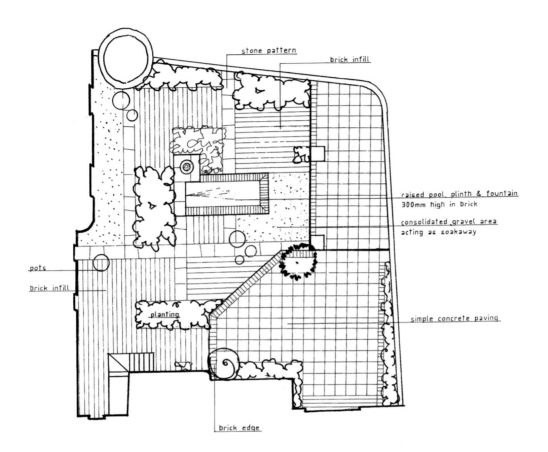

stone pattern

brick infill

raised pool, plinth & fountain
300mm high in brick

consolidated gravel area
acting as soakaway

pots

brick infill

planting

simple concrete paving

brick edge

In this garden, a raised pool of water and fountain is a central feature that provides the play of light and sound. It is balanced with masses of plantings and different paving treatments, including gravel. Kept simple, this garden will be low-maintenance but elegant and peaceful.

probably calls for a regular shape to work with a terrace's geometry, which in itself will probably work with the house. You are beginning to build up a relationship of shapes, which is what a garden's design is all about. Such a pool can be of concrete, sunken fibreglass or butyl rubber – tailored to fit the size of the hole you have prepared. (Rubber is guaranteed at least fifty years provided it is laid properly; earlier plastic sheets used for lining pools deteriorated far more rapidly where they were exposed to sunlight.) A regular shape of pool is much easier to detail at its edge as well, with brick, stone or concrete.

I have a personal dislike of small free-shaped pools, which never seem convincing – larger ones can look good and wild, but not I fear when constructed in fibreglass and in miniature. Throw in the plastic rock cascade and you are in noddy land in no time.

You might get away with a small pool by creating a large beach effect around it of mixed pebble sizes, with masses of willowy, watery plantings. For one of the many attractions of water is the usually large-leaved plant material that can be associated with it.

HOW TO DESIGN A GARDEN

Another attractive way to use water is as though it were a cattle trough. Where its surface is 50 cm/20 inches off the ground with a wide surround, it's good to sit on as well, to dabble your fingers and feed the fish.

I saw a nice idea on the Continent once, where instead of tubs of annuals on a terrace they had tubs of water, with different plants in each. (There was the added advantage of not needing regular watering.)

For many people a plot is not complete without a rose garden. As a designer I groan, for while the actual flowers of Hybrid Tea and/or Floribunda roses are superb, the plants themselves are not – and from autumn until late spring you look at a collection of no doubt beautifully pruned twigs. I think that you can relieve this situation in a number of ways.

First of all, roses don't need to be grown all on their own. I believe that they can be blended with herby subjects perfectly well, some of the sages, lavender and rosemary holding foliage interest through winter. They should not be grown through one another but in blocks – for roses need feeding and herbs do not.

Shrub roses mixed with smaller herbs or perennials can add interest by way of autumn hips and give a variation in height. If you are heir to one of those 1920s formal rose gardens (where the roses have probably had it by now anyway), intersperse some of the beds with perennials, even low shrubs, and you will create a far more interesting place to stroll through.

LEFT Small containers or pots of water with water plants growing in them is a manageable alternative to a pond, especially in a smaller garden.

RIGHT Roses can be grown with other plants to minimize their twigginess in winter.

## THE VEGETABLE PATCH

Increasingly I find that vegetables and a greenhouse don't spoil a garden, they enhance it. They can be worked into a larger garden – and in a smaller space too. I was brought up always having to hide the vegetables by siting them at the furthest point from where you wanted to use them, usually behind a rotting trellis – heir again to the generation that sent a servant to cut them, I suppose, so it didn't matter how far away they were! Now I appreciate the foliage of vegetables, mixed perhaps with herbs. And here there is a case for a logical squared layout, for the vegetable patches need to be of a manageable size.

I have seen in the United States prepared vegetable beds raised above ground level by 30 cm/12 inches or so by timbers. This way, particularly if the soil is poor, you can improve the vegetable growing potential by adding good stuff on top. The effect is of being among the vegetables much more. Add the odd arch for climbing beans and you can create a very stylish garden look, allowing lots of space for a greenhouse/garden shed and its surround, along with a compost area. Even bring in a raised pool for dipping your watering can.

Such a garden might, however, be without any grass. Which brings us to the merits of grass (or not, depending on your viewpoint).

A well laid-out vegetable garden, especially in combination with a greenhouse, can be an attractive feature. Remember that the veg beds should not be too deep or you will not be able to reach in and weed or pick your crops.

## GRASS

Some areas are fortunate enough to have a climate which supports grass easily. And for many years it was the most common medium for the floor of a garden. But increasingly the manufacturers of chemical feeds and/or weedkillers have persuaded us that just a mown lawn is not good enough – it has to be immaculate and as far removed from a natural sward as possible. A good lawn has now become another monoculture in fact, with the highest concentration of fertilizer, weedkiller and water of any other growing medium. And it needs regular mowing too. Of course, it looks superb and does provide a place to sit the baby, but at what cost? Lawn doesn't feature in the French, Italian or Japanese garden style. It doesn't even feature in the cottage garden – for if you are surrounded by fields of pasture, who wants another on your side of the hedge? One must ask whether the scale of a small lawn is worth its trouble – the little muddy place you see in winter? So perhaps there is an alternative to fill up your garden which will certainly give it a different style. Just longer grass, even a pattern – a chequerboard, for instance, of long and short grass might be interesting, with bulbs and/or wild flowers in the rough areas; a mown path through rough grass looks exciting. One problem is that you will probably need both a cylinder mower as well as a rotary to create these levels (more storage necessary).

Another alternative to lawn is low ground-cover planting, of periwinkle perhaps, or epimediums. Then gravel can be used as an alternative ground cover, or even bark.

Through these different mediums, which need laying properly, you can plant loose arrangements of shrub roses, shrubby herbs, even tall grasses to create a look that might initially shock the neighbours, for we are very conditioned by tradition to the way a garden should look. The use of more gentle plant material overlaying new forms of design layout creates, I believe, a style which is both of its time and – increasingly more important – of its place as well.

### TOP TIPS TO TAKE AWAY

1. Never forget that your lifestyle, as much as the architecture of the house and the local vernacular, should drive design decisions.

2. Make lists of your – and your family's – needs (and what you don't want) to guide you.

3. Be practical: recognize the limitations of your budget and your time.

4. And the fact that you'll need places to store the mowers, the dustbins . . . and the rest.

5. Although there are many different elements, from many disparate garden styles, you can incorporate in a garden, try if possible to avoid a piecemeal approach.

6. Above all, always remember that building up 'a relationship of shapes, which is what a garden's design is all about,' is essential in creating a cohesive garden layout.

7. And – 'less is more'!

In the late 1980s, Celia Haddon wrote in the *Express* that John's early gardens 'were a shock to the traditional gardeners, brought up to believe plants must come before everything else. You could sit in a John Brookes garden. You could hold a drinks party in it. And if you didn't like gardening, you could do very little gardening indeed.' In this charming article, John aims his advice at the homeowner who was inclined to do very little gardening, as he describes how one might create a garden that could be maintained with only one week's work spread out through the year. Among other things, he likens his approach to interior design and reminds his readers to link the interior and exterior with colour, plants and other elements.

## A WEEK-A-YEAR GARDEN:
## HOW TO GO ABOUT CREATING ONE

One of the joys of having a smallish garden space is just pottering in it a bit or deadheading, tucking the odd climber in, pulling the odd weed out, a touch of watering, glass in hand on a warm summer evening, and so on – half an hour here and half an hour there – it's amazing what gets done!

Now a week a year is actually quite a lot of pottering, for seldom does our busy lifestyle allow for a whole day out in the garden at a time. You might need a morning in late autumn to put the garden to bed as it were, but for the average good small garden that will be enough. While leaving plants with seedheads as food for birds in winter, there are other chores to do to ensure the health of your garden, including removing diseased plants along with any that have pest problems, removing tender bulbs that need to be stored, and adding compost as a mulch that can decompose during the winter.

But what is a good small garden and good for whom? There is the crux. Good for you is the answer, for gardens are for the people who use them (and have to maintain them); the smaller the space, the more important this is. We have been conditioned for so long to consider the garden as a place only for plants, which it need not be if you are overwhelmed by the whole horticultural 'thing'. A few well-chosen plants will, of course, bring an otherwise static setting to life, but you are not trying to distil the essence of a country garden to town house proportions for it won't work. You are trying to extend your limited internal space outside and to give yourself something decent to look at from inside for as much of the year as possible.

Indeed, the whole small garden concept needs a bomb under it for the average one is both dull and uninviting, and its design, if it can be so called, is either of an eighteenth-century idyll totally unsuited to a modern urban space or a sub-Japanese mishmash of railway sleepers and dwarf conifers, all beneath the harsh glare of a Victorian lamp post!

This small town garden includes seating, an overhead enclosure in the form of a simple pergola, and a modest amount of planting that is easy to manage. Aside from sweeping and possibly the occasional power-wash, the paved terrace is also a low-maintenance surface suitable for garden furniture, pots and even children's play.

It is very odd that many homes which are really beautifully designed internally come to a grinding halt at the window. Yet interior design – the arrangement of furniture within a room and of pictures on a wall, the selection of colour and texture of fabric with fabric – is very similar to putting all the elements of a garden together. One is thinking first of function and practicality (for which limited time for maintenance is part), then scale and styling, all conditioned by economics, to create a particular mood. It is just that mood which you seek to create outside.

What goes wrong is that so many think first of often totally unsuitable plants, and then hope to arrange everything around them. It's like designing a room around a lampshade, which can be done of course, but it's a 'putting the cart before the horse' sort of method.

So, start off by listing what it is that you want outside, long before thinking plants – some hard surface, perhaps, to stand the pram on; a terrace on which to have a drink in summer; some water. And admit to yourself if you have not the time, or even the inclination, to garden.

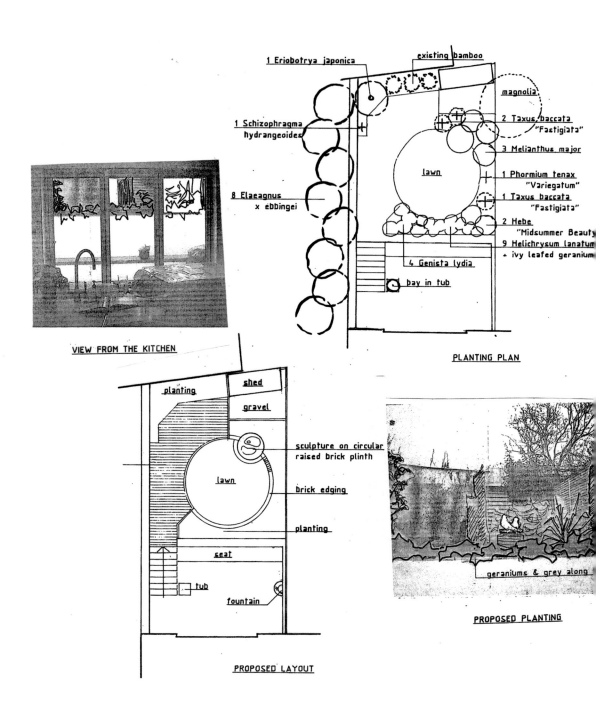

**1 Eriobotrya japonica**

**existing bamboo**

**1 Schizophragma hydrangeoides**

**magnolia**

**2 Taxus baccata "Fastigiata"**

**3 Melianthus major**

**1 Phormium tenax "Variegatum"**

**1 Taxus baccata "Fastigiata"**

lawn

**8 Elaeagnus x ebbingei**

**2 Hebe "Midsummer Beauty"**

**9 Helichrysum lanatum + ivy leafed geranium**

**4 Genista lydia**

**bay in tub**

VIEW FROM THE KITCHEN

PLANTING PLAN

planting

shed

gravel

sculpture on circular raised brick plinth

lawn

brick edging

planting

seat

tub

fountain

geraniums & grey along

PROPOSED LAYOUT

PROPOSED PLANTING

Keeping the garden simple though bold can bring the need for maintenance down and, just as important, ensure that it won't become a nagging chore.

Now think about scale and style. Broadly, the simpler the plan of the garden, the cheaper and easier it will be to build. This does not mean that it should lack subtlety, however. You will be thinking line and pattern in the same way you do when putting, say, six pictures together on a wall, when you relate each square or rectangular frame to each other, and then consider the whole mass within the perimeter of the wall surround with a chair or lamp in front of the group. This is a three-dimensional exercise which we all do inside.

In the same way, relate areas of paving to areas of gravel or planting or water, to the shapes and proportions of the surrounding walls or fences, and to the plan of the house they adjoin. Think in broad simple masses to start with: you should be thinking about proportional groups to fill in the whole pattern, for too many individual things – be they plants or pots – only fracture the overall scale. You do not, after all, cover each chair in your sitting room with a different coloured fabric. Mind you, there will be occasional specimens which serve a particular function, relating to a distant tree perhaps, or relating the garden plan to the height of the back of the house.

Now decide on the style of your patterning to be in keeping with the style of your house, its location, your interior mood, and how you will use the garden.

If you can create the same mood both in and out and make the spaces flow logically, you will be amazed at how much bigger each space seems, and then with subtle lighting and wall colouring you can bounce the imagery to and fro from in to out. Try using strong colours outside on walls, or tones of the same colour on different walls. Use *trompe l'oeil* – it doesn't have to be classical – think of those fun painted blank windows you see from time to time with painted silhouettes of people behind curtains: that sort of thing.

Above all, do not be timid. Scale up your concepts to be bold and theatrical. It usually works well outside, for while your two-dimensional plan might be small, your third dimension reaches up to the sky!

The harsh reality of economics might temper your wildest fantasies, but far better to start this expansive way and then scale everything down to reality than to work upwards from a mean garden centre level.

There is a strong relationship, of course, between the cost of your initial outlay in constructing a garden and its subsequent maintenance.

The traditional horticulturalist (gardener) will be snorting, 'typical landscape designer, hardly mentioning plants because of course he hates them, and probably doesn't know any'. Not true; of course, plants have a place within your week-a-year garden provided that you have the time and inclination to look after them. The point which I am trying to make is that a small outside space can be more than the sum total of the plants which you put in it – for like pets, plants need a commitment if they are to respond and fulfil their glossy photographic descriptions. It's the basic layout, its ingenuity and above all its scale and character in relation to its surroundings which I think so important – and most of all its relationship to you, its owner. A garden should not be a nagging chore, even for a week per year, and by overreaching yourself, often horticulturally, it can so easily become just that each time you look out of the window.

You can evolve a basic garden plan based on the scale of the portion of the house protruding into the garden. Many people start off a garden design in the classic symmetrical idiom – a path down the middle with a tit-for-tat balance on either side. This approach is difficult, if nigh on impossible, given the average asymmetric small yard layout.

The shapes in the garden should have a proportional relationship to each other and be simple, no matter of what you make them – planting, paving, water or whatever – and they in turn should have a proportional relationship to whatever surrounds the garden, like a wall or fence.

When I start to work out my final garden plan, and realize it in hard or soft materials, I will relate the shapes to the function of the garden – a place to sit, something nice to look at – and even relate the plan to the house interior as well. All will be in relationship to the sun, too. I might use a run of paving inside the sliding glass doors, not only to protect the carpet from summer comings and goings, but to provide a place on which to stand plants, so bringing outside in.

I might use a consolidated gravel surface, hard rolled, as an alternative to installing grass or completely paving a large area. Plants which self-seed can be grown in the gravel, and sculptural features might take the form of topiary.

In this garden, the shapes created by the paving and planting beds are enhanced by different paving applications and low walls, all of which are proportionate to the features of the house.

The garden should have styling in terms of colour and planting. To increase the inside with outside mood, I might continue the colour of an internal wall outside by painting an exterior wall or fence a similar shade, or even another colour, depending on the mood inside.

A specimen tree might be used, such as the yellow foliage *Robinia pseudoacacia* 'Frisia', sometimes known as the false acacia or black locust tree. It has feathery foliage of a lovely bright yellow turning to copper in autumn, and its roots are not too invasive. Beneath the tree could be a mass planting of the evergreen shrub *Viburnum tinus*, which is covered with white flowers through the winter months. The evergreen forms of euonymus, some of which are variegated, would be perfect for colder climates.

Massed annuals like deep yellow antirrhinums or white busy lizzies would provide a great blast of summer colour, and in winter there would be winter-flowering pansies followed in spring by either lily-flowered tulips or hyacinths, all of one colour, to keep the scale going.

Climbers could be evergreen ivies, gold-berried pyracantha (for the birds), yellow climbing rose 'Mermaid', some honeysuckles for scent, or the golden hop, a rampant annual climber.

The effect would be strong and simple. And it would need very little maintenance when established – a garden made beautiful by less than one week's work a year.

## TOP TIPS TO TAKE AWAY

1. Take the same approach to designing a small garden as you would to designing a room.
2. The simpler your garden plan, the easier and less expensive it will be to build and maintain.
3. Relate the various areas of your garden to its shape and in proportion to the building and other elements that surround it.
4. Your garden style should relate to that of your interior.

Bulbs like these lily-flowered tulips can be used in single-coloured masses for a strong effect.

It was rare for John to be called into a project before a house was built, or even completed. Here he makes the argument that clients are better served when the garden or landscape designer is brought in at the beginning to ensure that house and garden are well integrated. In his memoir, *A Landscape Legacy* (2018), he recalls visiting a site in Patagonia at the beginning of the project. The house was to be built on the shores of a tremendous lake with the even more tremendous Andes rising high above it. He writes:

> *The house had been pegged out, and much to the architect's annoyance (though he was nice enough not to show it), we laid out all the rooms with tape so that the clients could walk through them and imagine the view that they'd have from inside the house. I believe that the views from inside the house are every bit as important as the views one has from inside the garden, but in my experience, clients very often don't realize this to start with.*

Although he believed that garden design and architecture should be complementary disciplines, they all too often are not, to the detriment of the client.

## WORKING WITH ARCHITECTS

My views on garden design and architecture as complementary disciplines are both mixed and contradictory, I'm afraid.

And what it comes down to is: who is the garden designer and who the architect? We often have different styles ourselves and it's the client who brings us together.

You see, there is a pecking order. It's a very enlightened client who gets the landscape architect to the site first, to site the house, put in shelter trees, and consider the drive. Usually, the architect gets there first and not only uses up all the money but starts dabbling in what he knows little about.

For at the end of the day I think that landscape design is far more organic than architecture. We are concerned with landforms, earth and plant material – and it's a very different sort of discipline to that of the architect.

Which doesn't mean to say, of course, that each profession cannot have some understanding of the other. With more understanding, I believe our wires would not get crossed so often. On balance, while these disciplines should complement each other at the design stage, I believe they seldom do.

Having said that, when one looks at older buildings, their setting is often superb – but time, I think, is a great mellowing agent and the one remaining tree – of what was perhaps once a large plantation – can look just right against a certain building. Even lack of maintenance can give a gentle effect to too hard an architectural concept.

Perhaps the crux of it all is the concept of the building in its setting.

I think what is complementary between building and garden, or what ought to be, is an underlying proportion in the design. This welds the two together more than anything – and results in the client or user happily moving between the two. Then the well-proportioned garden needs styling to work with the structure of the house – so that the materials of each are complementary.

Lastly, I believe that certain plants look right in certain places for they have a style, too. And these will weld not only the house into the garden but the garden into its location.

Landscape designers and architects often take different things into consideration. In this project, John was called in as the house was being sited and was able to ensure that specific views (which suggested placement of windows) and other considerations were taken into account before the architect began designing.

# ADVICE TO DESIGNERS

John was an acute observer of architecture and landscape design. In this 1990 lecture at a 'Plant Professionals Symposium' in the USA, he likens the evolution in landscape and garden design to that in architecture, suggesting that both change for the same reasons. He applauds what he sees as the rise of regionalism, which frees both architects and landscape designers from the 'tiny though universal palette', advises designers to look for the essence of the place in which they are working and to reinterpret this essence in their designs and planting. He asks: 'The people, the cars, and the function may be the same but need the landscape be as well?' He concludes that designers should be looking for new techniques of landscape design, construction and maintenance that can help solve the environmental issues that are of growing concern.

Designed by James Corner Field Operations, Diller Scofidio + Renfro, and Piet Oudolf, New York City's High Line is free of past traditions and approaches. It is a 2.3-km/1.45-mile park that successfully combines history (a defunct spur of the New York Central Railroad) and environmental concerns (native plantings and water features) with its setting (urban views).

## OUT OF THE STRAITJACKET OF STANDARD SOLUTIONS

There is an old saying that there is 'nothing new under the sun', a sentiment with which I do not entirely agree, for I believe that styles in most things do move along as we do ourselves. We could not possibly be called Victorian or Edwardian, which does not mean, of course, that much of our thinking is not based upon the ground which they trod previously. So, experience is cumulative, and history must be only one of the sources of that experience.

Another component of our current thinking must be our lifestyle. Let's consider what those two words encompass. It has a lot to do with the way we live – our homes, our cars, what we buy in the supermarket, and the fact that we travel distances for both work and holidays. All these factors we take as the norm, but in fact they change very quickly.

As a backdrop to these physical manifestations of contemporary living there is a philosophical process going on as well. One which through the media carefully manipulates our thoughts, not only to the right soap powder or chocolate bar, but which more subtly maneuvres the social aspects of our lives. A reflection of this philosophical process at any one time is the literature that we read, our paintings and our sculpture.

A much more concrete synthesis of both the philosophy and the practicalities of contemporary living is our architecture: the form of the buildings and of what they are made. One school of thought is called Functionism, which has as much to do with the way people use the structure as the material of which it is made. Fine steel, sheet metal and increasingly sophisticated glass techniques give the contemporary building a no-nonsense refinement, and a new style, based on the historical precedent of what people want and how they move, and realized by the architect in the materials of the moment. Such a structure is a synthesis of both old and new, practical and aesthetic.

But anything innovative inevitably causes a backlash for we are a conservative lot at heart. If the forward social pace is too swift, it seems to create a reciprocal backwards movement so that accompanying the Functionist style in architecture we have a return to the basic symmetry of classic architecture and neoclassicism, sometimes pure, sometimes not – for we can't resist inserting our own statement of the period.

I am dwelling at some length on pure architecture as an expression of all the social mores of a period, and I hope that you are beginning to wonder where landscape fits in. The point I am endeavouring to make is that landscape accompanies all these other stylistic changes, and it evolves for exactly the same reason.

Being at the sharp end of landscape practice we tend to forget or overlook what these accompanying influences are as we look progressively forwards for perfectly valid economic reasons, but often I suspect we need to substantiate where we are and why.

As there are different styles in architecture there are in landscape design as well. We, too, have a classical precedent in the European gardens of Italy and France, one which became overlaid with horticultural expertise in the late nineteenth- and early twentieth-century gardens in England.

But while we in England wallowed in nostalgia in the garden of the 1920s, those in the States and elsewhere had taken on board the modernist movement of the 1930s which started in Germany but with the advent of Hitler moved to Britain and the USA. In California it overlaid a previous Spanish internal courtyard concept of the mission house.

This early modernist movement was based on Bauhaus architecture, which had been influenced by the Japanese house and its close integration with the garden. Painting was abstract and people were introduced to assymmetry, and sculpture was organic or free form.

The new Californian garden of the 1940s was a synthesis of these influences, emanating from the Bay Area of San Francisco and epitomized in the work of Thomas Church. These gardens and later the landscapes which followed by James Rose, Garrett Eckbo and Dan Riley were truly innovative of their period when for the first time the car, the sliding window and the swimming pool – all twentieth-century innovations – influenced the look and workings of the layout.

The Donnell Garden in California includes Thomas Church's iconic swimming pool, and epitomizes the modernist approach to outdoor living that early in his career strongly influenced John's own views on garden design.

Rebuilding in Europe after the Second World War influenced the look of landscapes, when the design emphasis moved from private to public spaces. Concrete became the medium in which to build, not the refinement of the early modernists, but often a Brutalist full frontal attack. In the States the corporate building and its prestige landscape, designing acres of car park, became the vogue – the monolithic airport structure followed.

But from the 1970s, with a reaction against the high-rise and the advent of the town house, the scale of much housing has decreased, as well as the lots on which they sit. The style of house has changed too. We have become concerned with vernacular architecture and more natural materials; wood and stone are used in the structures, giving the house a greater sympathy with its surround (provided the wood and stone are sympathetic to the area).

Now this concern for surround is very important – for the word environment began to creep in and with it an interest with ecology and the place of flora and fauna. Our diet has become more organic and earth based. An organic diet is a chemical-free one and all these influences work upon landscape design. This is a pretty simplistic chronology – but I think the message reads clear. What is it saying to you? At what point do you tire of the universal palette from which we draw for our hard landscaping?

Slowly, very slowly, regionalism is developing: that is, landscapers are seeking to integrate their developments into their surrounds. It's a sort of humility, though a pride of place too. After all, there is no reason why a factory surround in South Carolina should look like one in Boston or Los Angeles; we should be looking for the essence of each of those places and reinterpreting that in landform, in planting and in paving. The people, the cars and the function may be the same but need the landscape be as well?

Slowly, I hope this mood reduces the influence of the English garden – of course, its influence will be there historically – but the North American perennial pastiche of it must cease. The irony is that many of those perennials – the asters, the goldenrod and all – are your natives.

Which brings me back to the wild again. New approaches to landscape design seek to reinterpret wildness, held and strengthened by design techniques modern or traditional, to serve a usership on whatever scale, public or private – all honed by the practicality of maintenance – and, I suppose I have to say it, cost.

Practicality and cost, you will notice, at last creep in – but they always have and always will be the limiting or rather conditioning factors of a landscape composition. Without practicality none would have survived from last year, let alone last century. And a cost factor can change an overindulgent scheme to being a practical working reality.

So we are looking for techniques of landscape design, construction and maintenance which reflect this social concern for specific environments, on whatever scale. Some of the solutions have national identity, some regional and some purely domestic. This can at last get us out of the straitjacket of standard solutions, making each work an expression of its own particular place.

If a client wasn't happy, neither was John, for it was the pleasure and happiness a client found in the garden he designed that for him was the ultimate sign of its success. It was important to him to help homeowners develop their own gardens so that they derived the most pleasure from the outdoor extension of their homes. To this end, he begins here by emphasizing that 'horticultural excellence' is not the key to making the most of one's garden. In fact, planting comes last in the process. Determining the homeowner's needs and desires, the site's attributes, limitations and potential, and the appropriate style of the space and materials that link garden to home and setting are fundamental starting points. After getting the feel of a site and once decisions are made, the designer should be ruthless about taking out anything that gets in the way. John emphasizes the importance of developing a scaled design on paper and reminds the designer that the planting should be kept simple and include reliable plant material rather than difficult to maintain exotics.

## CREATING A GARDEN THAT SUITS THE CLIENT'S NEEDS

Many people think, I am sure, that designing is all imagination and fine feeling: a matter of selecting with taste from the vast range of plants available, paying careful attention to the way colours harmonize and contrast with one another and to the pattern of seasonal change. That is quite a mistaken idea of my kind of designing. Plants are not the only thing, or for that matter the first thing, I think about. What I want to create is a garden that suits the needs of the people who are going to use it. Before I put anything on paper, I want to hear from them. Clients who want to offload on the designer the job of working out the priorities really make me angry. To simply say 'you know best' leaves a designer like me missing the essential information for working out a scheme.

The modern garden has to take account of our modern lifestyle. The gardens of the past are, of course, rich in ideas for us, but whatever we take from them has to be interpreted in terms of the way we live now. An important factor is the amount of time available for looking after a garden. Our gardens are shrinking but so is the amount of time we have, and there are many leisure alternatives to pruning roses and digging potatoes.

Partly because they are shrinking, partly because of changes in lifestyle, gardens are required to satisfy many functions, of which the display of plants is only one. And what we want of a garden is not going to remain constant throughout our lives. For young people without children the need may be for an open-air area that can be used for relaxing and entertaining. For a family with small children the priority will probably be the provision of play areas that can be easily supervised. As the children get a bit older a larger area might be

By remembering that the garden is an extension of the home and thinking its layout through before you start creating it, you will find that the garden becomes a place that fits both your client's style and lifestyle, even as they evolve.

devoted to growing vegetables, and when they have grown up there may be more time and inclination for growing ornamental plants. A point is reached, however, when management becomes a burden if the planting and the layout are not simplified. Throughout all the phases in an owner's life the garden can serve as an extension of the house, and the more relaxed the feeling it creates the better. We have to get out of our minds the notion that horticultural excellence is the only standard by which a garden should be judged if we are going to make the most of our small spaces.

The very ordinary day-to-day aspects of our lifestyle need to be taken into account right at the beginning. Perhaps there has to be room for car parking, or you may even want to consider erecting a garage in a position with easy access to the house but not so that it will gobble up the best part of the garden. A space has to be found to store rubbish where it is easily reached but out of the way, and the same applies to storing equipment and furniture that need to be put away during the winter months. If the service features of a garden are not thought out right at the beginning, it is very difficult to fit them in efficiently and inconspicuously. Their location will determine where you need to lay some of your hard surfaces.

Finding a way of satisfying the needs of those who are going to use it is the first step in designing a successful garden, but there are other general points to consider, too. It is important, for instance, that it should belong to its physical setting. In towns the landscape is so cluttered by buildings that the natural environment doesn't have to be taken into account to the same extent, so there is the opportunity for a kind of theatricality that would be quite out of place in the country. Equally, a country garden loosely structured and cottagey strikes a really false note in a setting that is dominated by urban bricks, stone and concrete. Where there is a feeling of the natural landscape, that is something to take into account in your equation. If you can use local materials – and you can get a good idea of what they are by looking at older buildings and gardens in the area – so much the better. To get them you may have to go to some trouble; garden centre merchandising of plants, materials and equipment encourages uniformity and standardization. If you can't get local materials it is worth trying to obtain them second-hand.

In many cases the house for which the garden will be an extension is already a mature element in the landscape. The design of the garden and the materials used must be in sympathy with it. In many gardens it is the transitional area close to the house that requires the most careful treatment, matching materials – brick to brick, for instance – or at least using materials that combine happily.

Establishing the link between the inside and the outside of the house is something that has been learned from countries with a warm climate, but it

The materials used here in this small garden link the garden with its surroundings as well as the materials of which the house is built. A terracotta urn adds an exotic touch that does not feel out of place.

In gardens where interior and exterior spaces flow back and forth through large windows and open doors, especially in warmer climates, it is especially important that the colours and details of both the interior and exterior are complementary and harmonious.

is just as valid in cool, moist ones. A floodlit snowy garden in winter is an important visual, although not as practical as a sunny terrace for eating out in summer. The link can be strengthened by the use of decorative or structural elements that cross the threshold. My own dining room at the Clock House opens on to a paved terrace with overhead beams that are stained to match the wood of the doors. The use of plants in containers inside and outside also helps to bridge the divide so that one area melts into the other.

If the house is mature some sort of garden is likely to exist already. It should be viewed in the same critical way as a new piece of ground. Does the garden as it exists meet the client's requirements? Are there features of it that could be incorporated in a scheme more suited to their needs? Is it worth considering your first ideas in the light of outstanding existing features, such as a good stone or brick wall? As in all aspects of the preliminary stages of designing, you have got to take time to get a feel for what is there and appreciating how best it can be used. But once you have made your decision and are clear about what you want, you may have to be ruthless. One is naturally reluctant to move trees and shrubs, but if they are badly positioned and can't be moved, they may have to be cut down.

Whatever the size of the garden, you need to get a plan on paper before making changes on the site. The easiest way is to begin with a rough sketch of the area on which you can record the measurements as you take them. You can then transfer these measurements to a plan drawn to scale – preferably one to fifty for a small garden, although for something larger it may need to be one to a hundred. Mark the scale on the plan and also the direction of north, for you will need to bear the sun's direction in mind when laying out the garden. Make sure that windows, doors and all existing features are recorded, and it helps to include those outside the garden's periphery that are significant, for example buildings and trees, because they cast shade. Once you have got an accurate record on paper you can begin to be more specific about allocating areas. If you use gridded paper, it will make it much easier to get an accurate idea of the proportions and pattern of your design.

There are a few general points to consider as you are mapping out your plan. The distribution of sun and shade is always important in the garden, one of the difficulties being that there are a lot of elements competing for a position in the sun. Few vegetables will succeed in a shaded area, and under trees the competition for nutrients and water will also restrict the range of plants that can be grown. Ornamental pools, swimming pools and greenhouses all need open positions, while terraces and swimming pools need shelter, something that may have to be added in the form of hedges and fences.

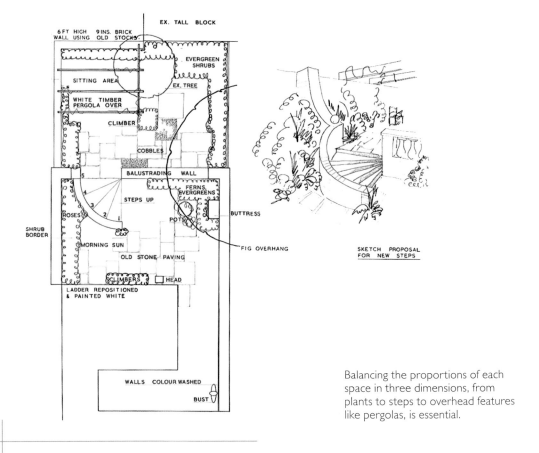

Balancing the proportions of each space in three dimensions, from plants to steps to overhead features like pergolas, is essential.

Privacy is another factor that has to be taken into account, although it is not worth getting obsessive about if to achieve it other aspects of the garden are going to suffer. A mistake that many people make is to work from the boundaries in rather than from the house outwards, so that the garden becomes a curiously isolated pocket and features outside it that could add to its interest and beauty are lost. At Clock House, the former stable block of Denmans, my half-acre garden flows into the three-acre garden created by Mrs Joyce Robinson. The only boundary between the two gardens is a drive.

All or part of the garden may be suited to a symmetrical formal arrangement, as might be the case if it is attached to a period house of symmetrical architecture. However, a less formal design allows for more flexible treatment of the various units that go to make up the garden and can help to create a more relaxing environment. But when there is no symmetry, there must be a sense of balance and proportion. Without it a garden will be an assembly of parts that don't make a coherent whole. A small garden, in particular, is a like a piece of sculpture, where there has to be a balanced proportion of bulky masses and voids.

Plants are the main constituents of the garden that transform a two-dimensional scheme into something in three dimensions, and for that reason alone they are important. But I have to keep stressing that making a fascinating collection of plants and growing them to perfection is only one kind of gardening. It is very satisfying for those who enjoy it, but there are many who want an agreeable outdoor room and are not especially interested in the vast range of cultivated plants available. They want reliable and attractive performers rather than the specimens that excite the plant enthusiast.

Your planting scheme has to take into account the growth rates of plants. Trees may take many years to reach maturity, but even shrubs will take three or four years to fill out, and in the meantime you might consider using short-lived annuals, biennials or perennials to give bulk to the planting in the first few years. The life cycle of plants ensures that the garden is never static.

## TOP TIPS TO TAKE AWAY

1. The first and most important step in designing a successful garden is to satisfy the needs and aims of your client.

2. The garden you design should feel at home in its physical setting.

3. The design and the materials used must be in sympathy with the house and the locale.

4. Identify the outstanding existing features that you want to keep, such as a good stone or brick wall, and be ruthless about removing what doesn't work, including existing trees and shrubs.

5. Get your plan on paper, including your site analysis, before you begin designing.

6. Balance and proportion, on both the horizontal and vertical planes, are vital, especially in an asymmetric scheme.

7. Plants transform a two-dimensional scheme into a three-dimensional design, so use plants that perform well and take into account their growth rates.

In a few words, John outlines for his students in Buenos Aires the first meeting with his clients and the ensuing design process. In effect, this is just as important for the client to understand as it is for the prospective garden designer.

## MEETING THE CLIENT

It always seems to come as a surprise to clients that I do not go into a new job and lay down the law. I only compute the facts, which are:

1. What the client's brief is to me – that is, what do they want from their garden?
2. What the house is saying to me – that is, is it traditional or modern, what is it built of, and what is its style?
3. What the site says to me – that is, what do the weeds tell me about the soil, how do the sun and wind affect the garden, what are the views?

I then say I want to work *with* my client to produce a plan – not *for* them.

First, I produce a sketch proposal. If they like that and want to build the garden, they get detailed structural drawings and a detailed planting plan. When measuring up the site I do an analysis of the location bringing together 1, 2 and 3, and it goes over the survey.

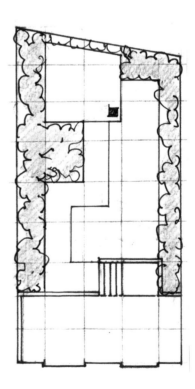

I then evolve a basis for my pattern taken off the proportions of the house – it is called a building module from which I evolve a design grid. Within any set grid I can evolve a garden pattern to fulfil all the requirements.

Now a garden plan is a sort of collage of shapes that have to be tempered by practicality. I work two-dimensionally on a plan but think three-dimensionally, considering levels and heights as I go along – it's sculpture as opposed to painting. And the other difference in landscape design is that one also has to take into account the fourth dimension, which is time: time and growth.

After my basic layout I complete my planting plan. It is a matter of putting plants in place to allow them to come together to create a mass over a given period, say five years. Increasingly I am doing very loose plantings the natural way, getting away from the huge border approach and planting in a gravel mass.

The relationship between the interior of a house and its garden is not always recognized by homeowners or designers, a failure that often leads to design disaster. John encouraged his students to be sure to meet with the client inside their homes before proceeding outside. Spending time inside helps the designer to understand which views are most important, to get a feel for the client's style, and to help formulate ideas about the connection of inside to outside.

Just one more thing to think about – style.

## THE RELATIONSHIP BETWEEN THE INTERIOR AND EXTERIOR

The styling of a design is, I admit, a bit of a slippery slope since it is so personal, and as a garden designer one is trapped between the style of the house and the location – one interprets a style to suit both.

So, the period of the house and what it is built of, the location, whether urban or rural, will affect not only the 'look' but the orientation of the site, and its soil will affect the subsequent selection of plant material.

But there is another aspect which is important: that is, the style of the interior from which you view the garden. Most interiors are, one has to say, fairly middle of the road but occasionally you come across a beautifully designed one as well. I think that the garden designer has to be aware of interior styles, for it is from them that you proceed to the garden.

This is the bit which I really enjoy, and it is in finding a solution to this problem that one uses all one's experience.

LEFT When producing a sketch of the garden, remember the design begins as a collage of shapes that will be developed into actual features, from storage to terraces. If you are working with a designer, be prepared to articulate what it is you want from your new garden.

RIGHT Look at the garden from inside the house and try to use the interior style in the design of the garden. Views from a window can be used to complement the interior in many different ways.

From early in his career, John was concerned about the environment and sustainability, though he might not have used that term in the 1960s. He was markedly influenced by Rachel Carson's 1962 influential book, *Silent Spring*, which he said 'was a tirade against humankind's attempts to use technology to dominate nature and it moved conservationists, in their relatively narrow groove, into the wider world of environmentalism. It helped to motivate a sweeping social movement that has since impacted almost every area of daily life.'

In this piece, John observes that gardens are trending towards smaller outdoor rooms with a more relaxed structure. While reminding his audience that the simpler the garden, the greater the need for a structured design, he also suggests that there is a need to reconnect with nature in the garden as development erodes the countryside. He presciently says that plant breeders will create simpler plants, a concern now as some hybridized plants are inaccessible to pollinators, and emphasizes that designers should learn to work with the land rather than to attempt to change it. Though speaking to an audience of designers in 1998, his words remain highly relevant.

## WHAT WILL BE CLASSED AS THE GREAT GARDENS OF THE FUTURE?

I am often asked what will be classed as the great gardens of the future, and I think it is difficult to say. What they thought of as a great garden earlier in the twentieth century will not necessarily be a suitable prototype for the twenty-first. Those nineteenth- and twentieth-century estate gardens relied heavily upon structure, but few now can afford this outlay, and using plant material alone, particularly perennial, is a much more transitory approach. The idea that great gardens are made to last may be challenged.

There have been huge social changes over the past hundred years and the great gardens of today are on a much smaller scale. The concern of the contemporary garden is now more to provide an ambiance for both the house and its surrounds and the family it serves. It is less about power and prestige. Often these newer smaller gardens are never open to public view, perhaps because of a fear of damage or theft, though in many places it is possible to see all types of gardens when they are generously opened to the public, often to raise funds for charity.

I think that in the coming years there will be further changes in garden aspiration. It's beginning to happen already. There will still be great collections of plants, however, and there will be formal gardens needing frequent and painstaking care, because the activity of gardening is still a pleasure to many. But there will also continue to be a more flowing type of garden whose plantings

The elaborate and labour-intensive flower borders and large gardens of the past are being replaced with smaller gardens that suit busier lifestyles and more limited budgets.

are less inhibited than those in the show pieces we have come to expect and which will relate much more closely to their location.

The terrace, barbecue and space for storage will require a 'room outside' adjacent to the house, but the remainder of the garden will, I believe, be less lawned (of the striped sort anyway). Increasingly, planting will be native to the locality or at least it will be suited to local conditions, since the challenge of growing plants well in environments that they find extreme will lose some of its potency. The overall feel will be more organic and free, with natural looking areas of water for birds and wildlife – and lots of winter interest providing hips and berries for food at a time of scarcity.

Herbs and choice vegetables will still be grown in limited amounts, but in a manner which harks back to the tradition of the cottage garden mixed together with the odd fruit tree. Plant breeders will, I believe, produce less elaborate flowers, and we will look again at the species and appreciate their simpler qualities and fragrance. They are, of course, more in sympathy with native plants from which many of them have been bred.

But the simpler the garden is and more random the planting, the greater the need for structured design beneath it. Design will move in a different direction, presenting an interface between a sort of shattered classicism and the ecological ethic. Environmental art will have its place as well.

For it makes sense as our countryside comes under increasing threat of development that we try to recreate in our gardens the feel of what has been lost. Do we need a universal suburbia fed by garden centres all selling a similar selection of merchandise?

I think there is an increasing place for wildlife and country centres which could demonstrate the use of native plants, and how to blend them with suitable garden types. They could introduce the city dweller to a real empathy for the 'country' – not romanticized or presented as a summer halcyon – and show how they can evoke it in their own garden.

Such a venue might illustrate the differences between gardening and managing the land, scaling down this process to the homeowner. The time is ripe for a greater emphasis on our husbandry of the land. We should no longer seek to change it for we are part of it.

There was a time when the garden designer had an elitist ring to his title, and the old gardener saw him as poaching his preserve, as it were. As gardeners, it was felt that we knew about garden design anyway – indeed we

Gardens that are simpler and more environmentally appropriate still need to have a well-thought through and executed design.

did and still do have a remarkable knowledge about garden plants and their care, but this has less to do with garden design now and, curiously, less with environmental issues.

So, while we still treasure our traditions, there is an increasing pressure to move forwards and really face environmental issues, and the garden cannot be excluded from this discussion. With the garden goes the industry which supplies it: the growers, the manufacturers and so on. Do they lead their market, or do they respond to it? All too often it is the latter, I fear, and what we are fed is a mishmash of sentimentality as heritage charm.

I suppose that it is in town where it is seen as being most difficult to garden the natural way. But the soil is the same and the sky is the same – the top and bottom of it – wherever you are. And if you leave your garden for a week or ten days, nature very quickly makes herself known. Unfortunately, we never leave the garden to itself long enough, for what grows first are pioneer invaders. It is only with time that more natural associations would develop that are right for your soil and situation.

I am not suggesting for a moment that this is the way ahead – but it is an interesting supposition. There is a happy mean in there which we need to examine.

Gardeners and garden designers have a a responsibility to create gardens and to garden with the environment and sustainability in mind.

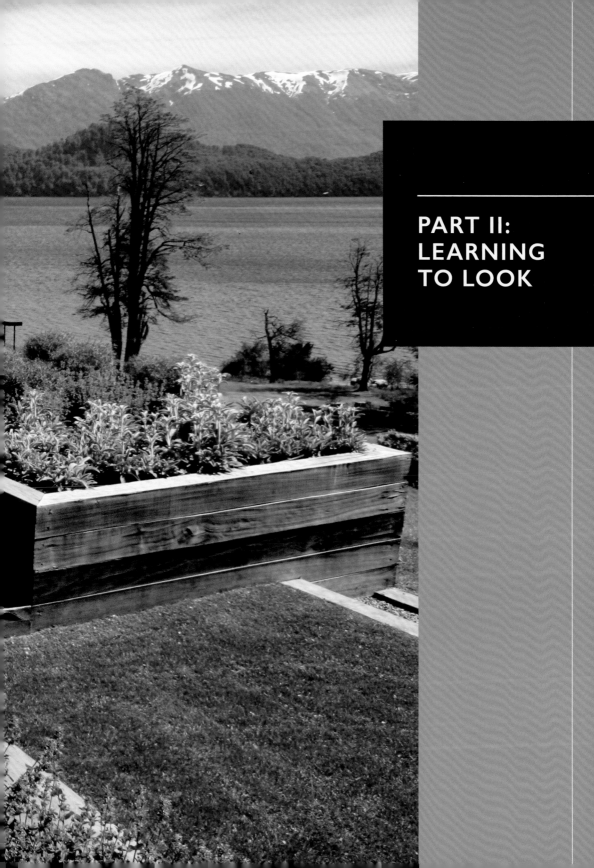

# PART II: LEARNING TO LOOK

# ON THE GARDEN IN ITS SETTING

John loved going to a new site and connecting with new clients, many of whom he counted as friends. He loved the challenges each new location presented, writing in his autobiography, *A Landscape Legacy*, that 'It is to the form of the landscape, or of a garden, that one instinctively reacts, and the interesting questions are: how much do you impose upon that form and what do you build it with?' These fundamentals never change: to create a perfect union between structure and architecture – the verticality of the buildings on the site and the horizontality of the design solution and its subsequent planting.'

He believed that by travelling and 'looking' he could bring more to the table as a designer, but, as he said, there is no place like home. Upon returning from his travels to Denmans, his home and garden in West Sussex, he would always say under his breath, 'East, west, home is best.' In this lecture to the Garden and Landscape Designers Association of Ireland, John admonishes his students that to connect with the 'mood of a site' – the surrounding landscape, the culture, the history, the plants – is to be able to celebrate it and, in turn, to help the client connect with the concept of 'home'. Again, this is just as important for the homeowner to understand.

The concept of 'home' becomes stronger when the garden is 'at home' in its setting.

## CELEBRATE YOUR SITE

I find that there is increasing media pressure which seeks to make one discontented and always want to be somewhere else, not helped, it has to be said, by foreign gentlemen showing glamorous slides of *their* gardens and landscapes! But believe you me, and I've seen a bit of the world, there's no place like home and our own cultural roots.

It's not incidental, I believe, that the word 'culture' is a component of the word horticulture, and those cultural roots are very deeply earthbound. That's why I called my contribution to today's symposium 'Celebrate your Site' – because part of the joy of being at home is enjoying where we live.

It was, of course, the physical condition of wetland, open land or woodland that traditionally shaped the type of agriculture that was practised in a particular place, and the society that lived off it. It also shaped the buildings in which people lived and the materials that could be used to build them – the walls, the fences and the gates of the landscapes as well.

In short, the elements shaped the landscape, and the garden was traditionally part of it. Poets, musicians, authors and painters celebrated where they lived, churches celebrated the local patron saints in festivals, foods celebrated the passing of the seasons.

There's a universal standard of glitz which is peddled that we as landscape designers should resist, for with environmental concerns we as designers need our inspiration to be site-generated – and I do not mean just in a selection of native plant material. We need to tap deeper into those cultural roots which make home ground so important to us.

Curiously, our own cultures are sometimes the most difficult to evaluate – we can't see the wood for the trees sort of thing. When we go as a visitor or, even better, as a consultant, we can read more quickly other people's ways of life and the landscapes in which they live, since their strangeness is what stands out.

But to pursue this further, it is not just the strangeness of one country to another which should engage us; it's the difference of one site to another within differing physical regions, within a small area, and, further still, between the sunny side or the shaded one, the top of a hill and the bottom. And it is at this point that we get into plant associations in terms of the specific site as well.

Getting into the mood of a site is a fascinating exercise, and to a degree it's a step which we all need to do in assessing or celebrating a place. If you drive or go by rail you get a feel for the landscape: its topography, flat or rolling, mountainous or cultivated, forested or wet. If you fly you really see land patterns: that is, field patterns and cultivation techniques. Now take a look at a survey map of the area. Note the names of villages. Look at field names. Foggy Bottom or the Warren tell you something. Pub names are interesting too. In my area it's the hop pickers, Barley Mow, the hurdle makers and so on.

Social history is relevant, and you can take it further by delving into parish maps and the local planning office. Who owned what? Again, the survey often tells you.

The traditional village or even farm buildings will tell you of the local vernacular. Did they build in stone which was quarried locally? Was it sandstone, limestone or hard granite? Or did they use field stone rounded from glacial action or water worn? If no stone, was there clay to use for bricks and tiles, even the daub over wattle or the cobb of the West Country? Now the wood: was it oak or beech or birch?

Go closer and, depending upon the soil and moisture content, consider not only the native trees but shrubs as well. What is evergreen and what is deciduous? Work on down to the perennials and the herbs.

Thus armed with a cultural as well as physical analysis of a site, focus on the job requirement and the client's brief.

One's jobs can be:
• to restore
• to work on the style
• to integrate garden with landscape.

The scale varies but the procedure can be the same.

It gets more interesting and exciting, I believe, doing it abroad.

It is essential to take into account the materials of which the buildings of a site are made, the plants that grow around and within the site, and its cultural context, in addition to the client's needs, style and lifestyle.

# EXHIBITION GARDEN PLAN

scale 1/4" to 1'0"

**A**

6 ft. boundary wall.
verticals at 7'6" centres of 4' sq, 7'6" conc. posts
infill of circular concrete screen wall units (type A) No 15.
coping of 2' x 6' x 2' conc. slabs.

raised bed and incinerator contained
by 1 ft high x 8 inch conc wall. coping
round bed of 6" x 2" x 2" bull nosed, verge drip
asbestos tile (W/4193)

boundary wall solid panels.
verticals at 3'3" centres of 4' sq,
7'6" conc. posts, slotted vertically
to take 6' corrugated asbestos
wall cladding panels, painted, type A
(D/10571/C).
coping of 2' x 6' x 2' conc. slabs.

pergola - of 8' x 4' x 4" conc. verticals
with horizontals, of 8' x 4' x 4", dowelled
joints.

6" step up to paved terrace. Tread of
2" x 1' x 1' asbestos verge drip tiles (W/4193)
on conc. riser, continuing to form water
fall in pool. Mowing stone at step base
and round pool of 1' x 6" x 2' conc. slabs.
Terrace paving of 2' sq conc slab, in
4' sq sections of differing types,
marked by rubbing back joints.

pool at two levels, depth 18", water
flows over conc. step, and circulated
by garden pump concealed under
paving slab.

pavilion skeleton as pergola of conc.
posts 8' x 4" x 4" set in conc. floor
(coloured). Roof structure of
corrugated asbestos sheeting (Magnum)
W/5050 hung from steel horizontals
set in concrete skeleton. Fall to
pool of 1/2". Panels of coloured
asbestos suspended at rear of
pavilion to take exhibition of
submitted designs.

2' x 1' x 2" conc. slabs laid
12" below lawn levels and
forming pattern.

6" step up of 2" x 1' x 1' asbestos
verge drip tiles (W/4193) laid on
conc. risers.

solid boundary wall panels (orange)
asbestos flower boxes, type J
3 sections 15'2"  2 sections 9'2"

1' x 1' and 2' x 2' coarse aggregate
paving slabs.

I.L.A panels fixed to panel of wall

1 st. tree 15 ft.
(ash, sycamore)
2 cherry st. 10 ft.

evergreen shrubs 6'-7'
cotoneaster, rhodo.

raised bed for ease
of maintenance, herbs
lettuce or cut flowers

bush rose bed, all one
colour, underplant,
lavender, climber on
pergola

iris, rush, mace, in pool.

2 vertical st. trees.
20 ft., poplar.
6' evergreen shrubs
ivy on pergola

purple vine on pergola
1 st. cherry 10'
senecio laxifolius
hosta ground
evergreen 6'

rhododendron 5'

shrub roses 4' white

1 rhus cotinus foliis purp.
6ft.

3 vertical st trees 15'-20'
infill with herbaceous,
lilies, as available

6 silver birch 10ft'
6' evergreen (rhodo.)
silver ivy, with bluebells
foxgloves, lilies, as available

4 silver birch 10ft
with 6' evergreen
under (rhodo).

fill tubs with hydrangea (blue)
geranium (white) - as
available

**sculpture**

**terrace**

**step up**

**B**

**B**

pool

**A**

fall

**pavilion**

incinerator

raised
bed

**lawn**

**D**

step up

**C**

15'2"

9'2"

**C**

step up

RISE

**D**

John Brookes
2 Nottingham St, W.I.

In 1962, having won a competition to design an exhibition garden for the Concrete and Cement Association, John became the first *independent* designer to show a garden at London's Chelsea Flower Show. His exhibition garden controversially had less to do with plants than it did with creating a designed space for living, another first. His modernist garden featured the elements ideal for the 1960s lifestyle – a seating area, pergola, water, sculpture, modern furniture (made of asbestos, he liked to add with a chuckle) and even an incinerator. Though the use of garden space as an extension of the home was not new abroad, where it was popular from California to Sweden, the British were slow to embrace the notion. Despite his revolutionary presentation and the limited variety of plants, he won the Silver Flora medal. The following year, he wrote this article about designing small town gardens, which he likened to an outdoor room, a challenge he relished, though he much preferred country life.

## THE GENIUS OF THE PLACE: THOUGHTS ON GARDEN DESIGN

A garden to me is a retreat: this may sound mediaeval, but as city life gets noisier and busier, more than ever I am convinced that in a garden one should create peace. This should be visual as well as actual, and this retreat should invoke as many of the senses as possible. Smell, particularly by growing night-scented plants; touch, using textured plants as one might silk or velvet inside the house; and sound, in the play of water or even a canary in a cage: there is something fundamental and organic in all this which is important to human well-being.

It seems to me to be important to look at the garden from inside the house and to try to integrate the design and colours into the garden. A view from a window, which I see as the frame to the sight of the garden, can be compelling even in the finest interior. This internal/external flow of space and materials is particularly important when there is a large amount of glazing.

For me it is ridiculous, if one is to fulfil the requirements wanted of a garden, to impose a set style upon it – Italian or Spanish, for instance – styles which were conceived for a different climate and different ways of life. Equally, a plan copied from a book will not be successful since the author has no idea of his reader's specific wants.

One has to be careful not to get bogged down with planting details. Our enthusiasm for plants can wreck a design if not controlled. I leave plants as the last element of the design, in the same way as one would decide on pictures for a room after the carpet is laid and the position of the table and chairs decided upon. To rely entirely on planting as the backbone of a garden for the whole year is asking too much.

John's 1962 Chelsea garden was a 'room outside', designed to be a refuge from the demands of modern life.

To me, the differing factors entailed in the design concept of a town garden often make the town job interesting. It is perhaps perverse, but the more limitations to the space I have, the more satisfaction I get in producing a workable design for it. To design a garden in a small area is an exercise in space utilization rather than a horticultural frolic.

The amount of planting which one incorporates is up to the owner. In a small area, I prefer as few varieties as possible, but used generously where necessary. I restrict myself to a few all-year-round favourites for form, leaf shape and texture, with colour emphasis in pots. These can be changed regularly to keep them

fresh, or, if there is room, one can grow substitute pots which can be wheeled into place when necessary. Wooden tubs might even be on their own castors. I keep this sort of small-scale interest in the foreground, possibly on a paved area linked to the house, with the main background to the garden quite separate beyond. I keep to single colours per pot, perhaps picking up colour used inside the house, and blending or contrasting pots as necessary. In a small garden it is essential that the plants look their best all the time, with some form of interest throughout the year. It is for this reason that I keep the planting area fairly small.

For background planting I use a large proportion of evergreens for form, either in their leaf or overall shape. Particular favourites are fatsia, cotoneaster, camellia, mahonia and the occasional yucca. These I contrast with robinia, sumac, broom and buddleia. *Hydrangea paniculata* 'Grandiflora', potentilla, hosts, herby things – rosemary, lavender and thymes – are also useful. I love plants with grey felt-like leaves, but find them difficult in towns as they collect dirt and are unable to breathe. Through all these shrubs I plant lilies, Solomon's seal, lily-of-the-valley and lily-flowered tulips.

I find that lawns are not worth their trouble. In a confined space where there is no flow of air, they tend to become mossy and damp. Time and money are needed to keep them in top form if they are to be able to take any wear at all. Another thing against them is that small pieces of grass also tend to disrupt an otherwise calm area.

To me the town garden is an outside room that can be used for much of the year. A hard dry surface on which to walk is therefore essential. The actual type of material is often dictated by the site. Where there are brick walls containing the space, brick paving is an obvious choice to tie everything up.

Small gardens should be kept simple and uncluttered, in part to make sure that maintenance is manageable. Simplicity, however, does not exclude using water features or sculpture as long as they are in proportion to the design.

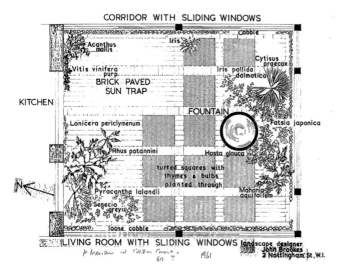

CORRIDOR WITH SLIDING WINDOWS

Acanthus mollis

Iris

Cobble

Vitis vinifera purp.
BRICK PAVED
SUN TRAP

Cytisus praecox

Iris pallida dalmatica

KITCHEN

FOUNTAIN

Lonicera periclymenum

Fatsia japonica

Rhus potannini

Hosta glauca

turfed squares with thymes & bulbs planted through

Pyracantha lalandii

Mahonia aquifolium

Senecio greyii

Loose cobble

LIVING ROOM WITH SLIDING WINDOWS landscape designer
John Brookes
2 Nottingham St, W.I.

1961

The plan above for the garden depicted on the left shows that it can be viewed from three sides from the interior. Making sure each view is interesting can be achieved by plantings, sculpture and paving materials, and the style of the outdoor details should be compatible with the indoor details.

York stone or blue stone tends to be dignified but a little unsympathetic when used to any great extent in small-scale surroundings. Certain types of tiles can be attractive in the right setting, as can granite setts. Different-coloured chippings are a possible substitute for grass and virtually maintenance-free. The important point to remember in choosing a paving material is that its elements should be in scale and sympathy with the surroundings. Avoid crazy-paving as it is fussy to look at, difficult to walk on and, when not properly jointed, difficult to maintain weed-free.

If the area is to be an outside room, it is important that the furniture should be sympathetic also. The two extremes to be avoided are the rustic bench, which is extremely cumbersome and out of scale in this context, and the pretty-looking little iron chair which is virtually impossible to sit on.

I am also interested in using stronger colour outside for walls, particularly in small town gardens which are not so much gardens in the true horticultural sense as an outside space with plants. Where the overall environment is green, one has to be careful in colour selection. Some of the lovely ochre colours of the Mediterranean would lend themselves well for walls, being cool in summer and warm in winter, and having the added advantage of not showing the dirt of smog so much. Used in conjunction with white woodwork and contrasted with purple and pale blue foliage and flowers, it could be very refreshing.

Generally speaking, I find that most of the difficulties in designing and making a garden are not in the area itself, but in the clients. Some have a fixed idea, which is so unsuitable; then there is the plantsperson who knows more about it than you do (there is a saying about keeping a dog ...); the people who can't decide and eventually change their minds at the last minute after consultation with the contractor; and lastly, the people who won't believe that no matter how much money they have, their plants will not grow any faster.

An ultimate idea for a garden takes time to mature, particularly when the design includes trees and hedges, and the right clients know that they will have to resist the temptation to change the plantings while waiting for them to achieve maturity.

Seven years after presenting his pioneering Chelsea garden, in 1969 John published his first book, *Room Outside: A New Approach to Garden Design*, which explained why the garden should be regarded and designed as an extension of the house, hence a 'room outside'. Ever practical and realistic, John coupled the relatively new idea with pragmatic and thorough advice, starting with design and moving on to the build and planting. John here presents the same concept to a Japanese audience, explaining further that the purpose is to create a beautiful, useable outdoor space that reflects the interior, arguing that in fact they should approach designing small gardens as exterior decoration but starting with a logical plan. As always, he suggests that plants may or may not be necessary.

## THE URBAN TERRACE AND SMALL GARDEN DESIGN

The title of my talk, 'Urban Terrace and Small Garden Design', really means making the most of a small space outside, and I am not sure that the word garden should come into it. For what I am really talking about is interior decoration outside – it's exterior decoration – the 'room outside'.

Such a space can be designed very architecturally, with coloured walls, overhead pergola structures or mirrors at odd angles. There might also be water for cooling and sound. It could be a magical outside room for summer dining and an extension of indoors, lit for late evening and winter effect as well. You will notice I have not mentioned plants – and, to be inflammatory, are they really necessary?

On the other hand, this outside room can be a little jungle, a green oasis in city life. If the room leading to your garden is exotic, has orchids, bananas and palms in tubs, you set the mood and style the garden as you would indoors. But, of course, since many of your plants in a town garden are in pots they will need more maintenance. For small town gardens are baking hot in summer, and roofs and balconies have the added dehydrating factor of wind. In addition to pots you can use window boxes and hanging baskets.

The small garden can be a magical place, but style it to your capabilities and the amount of time which you can spend upon its maintenance. Remember that the closer you are to your plants, the better their maintenance will have to be.

The process of designing a garden – however small, and the smaller it is the more important (like a small kitchen, much more difficult than a large one) – has to start with a logical plan.

Once the space is drawn to scale on a plan, you can fantasize and move elements about on paper to create the effect you want. You can price for the construction of the garden and decide exactly how many plants you want. So, measure the area first and draw those measurements to scale.

Now start to play about with pattern and shapes and the position of a table and chairs, which will define the width of a terrace necessary for them to stand upon. Decide upon how much soil area you want to plant, how much water, gravel, perhaps grass.

It is a sort of pattern you are making up, and at this stage it has nothing to do with plants. I am talking about the art of design – which is very different to the craft of horticulture and growing plants.

Once you have established a balanced pattern, start to clarify what each of the shapes is: first a terrace, then planted masses to surround the garden and give it shape, shelter and/or privacy.

If you have space, do you want grass? (Where to keep the mower?) Or should it be gravel – or even paved all over? Have you space for some water, a change of level and so on?

Would some shade be a good idea? An umbrella, perhaps, or what about a pergola?

At last, the planting. Think from the largest to the smallest, not the other way round. Is there room for a tree? Then the decoratives, the pretties, the infill: part of the infill will be your selection of pots, which you fill with annuals and bulbs for the spring.

Approach the design of a small garden in the same way you would a small kitchen, where every centimetre or inch is precious.

Part of connecting a garden with its setting is combining strong design principles, as one would anywhere in the world, and then using local plant material to connect the plant to its place. John was not a purist by any means; he used 'exotics' in his work but often theatrically, as an eyecatcher, or as part of the garden structure. He regarded native plants as a palette into which non-natives could be introduced, provided the native palette was understood. Nowhere is this more evident than at Denmans where natives mix seamlessly with exotics, each chosen for their attributes in the context of the rest of the garden. In this talk to an English garden club in 1994, John takes his point a step further here, however, by linking the garden to a modern lifestyle in which conservation and maintenance figure large as well.

## THE GARDEN IN ITS SETTING

I have purposely called my talk 'The Garden in its Setting' because I believe that in our headlong rush to achieve a sort of universal Sissinghurst look, we forget that Sissinghurst is a Kentish garden and Vita Sackville-West, creator of Sissinghurst Castle Garden with her husband, Harold Nicolson, was most specific about that.

Increasingly, I fear that with international marketing we forget the specialness of the place in which we have chosen to live; and in the garden, one of the places in which we could celebrate this, we still see its merit as being the number of exotics or alien plants we can cram into it.

Furthermore, being heir to past garden traditions, we plant them in the manner of the traditional herbaceous border in tight little clumps of three or five or seven – never even numbers for heaven's sake! But why? Nature doesn't distribute her plants like that. No one is cutting, lopping, pruning and spraying plants in the wild. 'Low maintenance' is the buzz word of the gardener yet we still perpetuate this technique of a forgotten age and, more importantly, of cheap labour.

So, this is my thesis: are we getting it wrong and should our setting have something to do with our plant selection and planting?

None of this negates design theory, which I believe is important, too. I believe it is possible to still think design in a layout, but by planting in a softer, more natural way one can achieve a more maintenance-free, more relaxed and more conservation aware garden that sits comfortably within its setting, rather than one which imposes itself to its own and everyone else's discomfort for miles around.

Combine a good design with more relaxed plantings to help minimize maintenance and be more environmentally friendly.

In an introduction to his design course in Buenos Aires, John exhorted his students to connect with their own culture and landscape rather than imitating the garden traditions of other countries. In an interview in 2006 with the British Library, John recalled taking his students out of the classroom and into the surrounding neighbourhood to teach them to 'look' – to see the indigenous plant material and landscape to help facilitate their understanding of their own 'local vernacular'. He reminded them that the Argentine landscape varied from one region to the next, and as his students came from these different regions, it was all the more important for them to learn to look at the landscape in which they were working.

Connecting garden to setting was a keystone of John's design philosophy and he taught it everywhere he went. He also practised what he preached, and consequently the gardens he designed abroad varied enormously not just from country to country but from site to site as well. In this 1994 lecture, the references to Argentina could be applied in principle to Japan, North America, Russia, Japan and anywhere else in the world.

As always, the lesson is relevant to homeowners, too.

## A PHILOSOPHY ABOUT DESIGN AND LANDSCAPE

First of all, let's kill the idea that as a Brit I am here to talk about English gardens. I am here really to explore with you what the new Argentinean garden may be like. It's a journey with you, not your client – for as designers we lead, not follow on. It might not feel like that sometimes for those of you in practice, but in the main it is true.

We all need to build up a philosophy for ourselves about design and landscape, so we are able to lead. Our course should be titled 'The Garden in its Setting'. And that setting is Argentina.

We have seen an increasing awareness of environmental issues, and the environment or the setting is becoming more and more important to the garden designer. The gardeners go on planting their roses and lavender, but we are beginning to question this. At the very lowest level I see that everyone here seems to be planting grasses and certainly this is grassland, but our approach needs to be more fundamental, I think. We should be considering land patterns (I am from the first generation to see our landscape from the air); we should be considering an often vanishing agricultural pattern; we should know our native plants; we should be aware of wetland within the environment, of woodland, of pampas, of the cold parts of the country and the hot dry parts. We should know the ecology of these areas and, within that, of individual plant associations.

At the heart of linking a garden to its setting is balancing environmental concerns and the local vernacular with a garden design that suits the needs of the people who use it. No matter where you are, looking at the surrounding landscape and taking into account the natural plantings, topography, and geology are essential exercises that will help you find this balance.

For into this we are developing our towns and cities fast, and we lose our landscape at our peril. Quite often we have been bewitched by grand gardens and gracious living which pay little heed to the native landscape. We should more realistically look at simple lifestyles, building styles and planting techniques of the people who are closest to the land and work up from that. I have recently seen exhibitions here that were in the main ignoring their Argentinean roots, so hell bent were they on being European and fashionable.

You must stop this and, through your gardens and landscapes, through your contacts with other designers, architects and decorators, show that there is an Argentinean way which calls on both historical precedent and vernacular style as well as modern innovation in its design.

Of course, there are rules to be followed – but I relate those rules to the musician's stave on which he can compose classical music or jazz. He can come off the top of the stave and he can drop off the bottom, but the melody always returns to the basic stave discipline. Garden design has its disciplines, too. I haven't mentioned either the client or his money (or lack of it more often), but they are part of the conundrum as well.

While his Argentine audience was highly influenced by Europe in the absence of an indigenous garden design tradition, John found himself conveying the importance of his 'garden in its setting' conviction to a Japanese audience with a slightly different twist.

Recognizing Japan's rich garden design history, he urged his students to seek a 'new Japanese small garden style' by reinterpreting Western design principles in conjunction with long-established Japanese traditions. Despite having designed the well-known Barakura English Garden in Nagano where he was able to isolate its Englishness from the Japanese landscape surrounding it, John is quick to point out that English garden ornament and features are largely out of place in most Japanese settings. His reference to a Tokyo roof is aimed at the English garden he designed on the roof of a Japanese department store.

## THE SPIRIT OF PLACE

I hope that it is not presumptuous of me to call the first part of my lecture 'Spirit of Place', for to us in the West the Japanese traditional garden is based upon this concept. It is a concept which, in a headlong enthusiasm to embrace Western gardening techniques, I fear that you might lose.

By spirit of place I mean an understanding and a reading of the elements which make up a landscape. These can be philosophical, mystical or more just an awareness of what we, with our 'conservationally' attuned antennae, would now call 'plant association' and 'habitat'.

It is the awareness of these facets of a landscape which your traditional gardeners reinterpreted in their small jewel-like landscapes, mostly in the temple setting.

By distilling the essence of a place, you increase its potency. By minimizing its components, the essence in the hands of an artist can be reduced down to a meaningful branch, even a single flower in an Ikebana arrangement.

It is this dramatic distillation of what is not shown and is only hinted at that makes so many Japanese traditional paintings so timeless and enchanting to the West and that influenced painters and gardeners like Monet. It subsequently got our early twentieth-century modernist designers to reject the decoration of the nineteenth century in art and architecture, and the classicism of the eighteenth century as well, and go on to produce a newer, cleaner line in building and design in general.

In rejecting classicism the modernists had, of course, 'thrown the baby out with the bathwater', for its rules and orders had been the basis of clear thinking in design since the time of ancient Greece.

It was the advance of technology during the Industrial Revolution which allowed new techniques in structure to be practised in the modernist mode and which produced some pretty startling buildings, and subsequently landscapes, too. Art and architecture were influenced as well by the new abstractions in painting and in art.

Modernism, and the International Movement as it subsequently became known, did not appeal to the imagination of the conservative British (actually the Second World War got in the way), and so a horticulturally attuned market filled the psychological gap left by the demise of a classical order.

By the late 1940s Britain was in a mess in more ways than one, for our designers were lost. We had rejected classicism on the one hand, and continental modernism had now turned into the slick International Movement of Chicago under Walter Gropius and Mies van der Rohe. This was a style totally out of character with the folksy British and, at the other end of the spectrum, to any spirit of place. We turned instead to cottage garden principles.

From the middle of the nineteenth century British gardeners had advocated a return to cottage garden principles, which came along with the Arts and Crafts movement, in itself a rejection of modernity and industrialization. But this was more a form of gardening rather than a style of design. It glorified vernacular architecture and native plants, too. It was another form of spirit of place – our British place!

Somehow, this early and mid-twentieth-century English gardening mode has been taken up by Japanese gardeners today. It is being introduced here, or at least its outward symbols are: the perennials of the herbaceous border, the Lutyens garden bench, the fey romantic statuary (a debased form of the classical). These are all perfectly legitimate in the English country garden, but I seriously question their appropriateness on a downtown Tokyo roof or in a small urban Osaka garden!

I would like to suggest that Japanese gardening style does not travel well to the West (although its principles do), and by the same token English cottage garden style does not travel well to humid Tokyo. Some Western principles can be applied here, but they need a reinterpretation to allow the emergence of a new Japanese small garden style which can express just as successfully as the old traditional way a truly new Japanese sense of place.

Just as elements of Japanese gardens can look out of place in Western gardens, elements of Western gardens can look out of place in Japan.

# ON GARDENS AND THE ENVIRONMENT

In 1962, the American environmentalist Rachel Carson published her controversial and influential book, *Silent Spring*. Though primarily concerned with the highly toxic chemicals that were being used in agriculture, it called attention to issues of environmental degradation and the need for conservation. The book influenced John significantly, though at first he did not make the connection with garden design.

When he first visited in Denmans in 1973, then owned by Joyce Robinson, he saw naturalistic planting in a structured setting, much of it in gravel. Though using many unusual plants, she made heavy use of natives, especially in the faux dry riverbeds she created in 1977–9. Recognizing that 'nature did so much of Mrs Robinson's work', her unique style intrigued him.

In time, the trend towards naturalistic planting and using natives appealed to him for three main reasons. As a practical matter, it is easier to maintain a garden when its plant material is not just native but is specific to the region in which the garden is located. Second, a garden is connected to its setting through the use of plants that grow locally. Third, he believed in the conservation aspects of using natives. He was not a purist, however, and did not hesitate to use 'foreign species' when it a served a design purpose. This was the 'middle way' for him as a designer and as a gardener at Denmans.

## NATIVE PLANTS AND THE ENVIRONMENT

There has always been a need to introduce and cultivate foreign species to an often alien soil. But why do we do it so assiduously? I can see that great landowners didn't need a wild garden. And why would a contemporary garden owner fill their plot with natives or what we used to call weeds? Somewhere, there had to be a middle way for the confused gardener.

When I trained in landscape architecture with Peter Youngman at University College in the 1960s, I do not remember the environment ever being considered; conservation was but certainly nothing eco.

My first initiation of an environmental concern, which to me didn't then have any direct influence on garden design, was when I read *Silent Spring* written by American author, Rachel Carson, published in 1962. This was a tirade against humankind's attempts to use technology to dominate nature and it moved conservationists, in their relatively narrow groove, into the wider world of environmentalism. It helped to motivate a sweeping social movement that has since impacted almost every area of daily life.

Visits to the US had made me aware of prairie landscapes, and more specifically of regional vegetation. I was much influenced by a book published in 1995 called the *Native Plant Primer* by Carol Ottesen, which defined the plant material of regions in the US, many of which are fairly vast, of course.

Earlier I had become aware of Mediterranean plants, and in both Australia and in South Africa I had seen gardens planted entirely with plants native to those countries.

For a period at Denmans I tried English natives, and more specifically I took on board what was growing locally in Sussex (not all of which are natives but were introduced from abroad some centuries ago). And of course, a huge range of our garden plants are hybridized versions of them. Just locally box (*Buxus sempervirens*) and yew (*Taxus baccata*) grow wild, with masses of shrubby viburnums, juniper, spurge, laurel (*Daphne laureola*), butcher's broom, cotoneaster (*Cotoneaster integerrimus*), sloe (*Prunus spinosa*), hawthorn (*Crataegus monogyna*), spindle tree (*Euonymus europaeus*), privet (*Ligustrum ovalifolium*), buckthorn (*Rhamnus cathartica*), roses – the sweet briar, the dog rose and the burnet rose – smaller trees including mountain ash (*Sorbus aucuparia*), birch (*Betula pendula*), and then forest trees, not to mention hundreds of herbaceous perennials, biennials and annuals with grasses and ferns.

I tried a number of these plants in the garden, but often found them too rampant and not really special enough. So, I got that one out of my system, though *Iris foetidissima* and the more common flag iris (*Iris pseudoacorus*), valerian, verbascum and lady's mantle still self-seed round the garden to my delight.

Combining native plants with non-native, even exotic, plants can add interest to a garden, but it is important to be sure that the non-natives are compatible with the soil and climate.

When I began to fly around the world and see the different landscapes below me, the different patterning of cultivation and human habitation, I started to realize how limited my horticultural vision had been. And I gradually became interested in the vernacular of an area, its materials and how they are used as well as its plants. It is this continuing interest which gives me an initial clue when I work in many different places around the world.

The dry riverbeds at Denmans include native and non-native plants combined to look natural and to provide interest throughout the year.

John lamented the disconnect between gardeners and the land, and here suggests that it is time for gardeners to learn from the landscape in order to regain the ability to enjoy their garden.

## LEARNING FROM THE LANDSCAPE

Looking at the road verges, fields and woodlands around your area will reveal what grows well locally, and guide you in making choices about what to include in your garden.

I think that we have become horticulturally attuned to fighting off nature – its bugs and droughts, its spots and its vermin – in the garden. We have lost quite often the knack and joy of being among plants and the pleasure of working with our hands in good soil (not 'the dirt' – that one sums up our contempt for nature, as though we had stepped in it and got it on our shoes). We have tried to sanitize the 'dirt' and improve it by throwing on expensive chemicals to make the grass grow and, when it's a few inches high, have a service in to mow it and blow it. Anyone coming from Mars might think us totally mad.

We should strike a bargain with nature and learn from it. Put away your manuals of horticulture for a moment and learn from your landscape.

Now on the premise that your garden is full of nasties which do eat everything, can I suggest you look very closely at your local woodland. It is not stripped bare, and all the nasties have free range. It has foliage, form and flower colour in season (a bit unkempt perhaps). Could it be that:

• you are growing the wrong things in your garden
• you are expecting too high and unnatural a standard
• you have lost touch with your roots – roots, notice.

But that is only to do with growing. How about the enjoyment of your garden as well? Learning to live in it – that is to do with design.

Entitled only 'Patterns – lecture notes', it is impossible to know when John wrote these undated notes and whether they were taken from a lecture he attended or for a lecture he intended to give, perhaps about Persian gardens. I think it was the latter, perhaps in preparation for a garden tour he conducted with Penelope Hobhouse through Iran. What is clear is that John's ongoing interest in pattern and form, whether found in nature or art, was profound and broad.

## PATTERNS

One of the concerns of a landscape designer must be visual patterns and forms in the natural world, for it is into the natural world that we insert our landscape plan, superficially urbanized though it may be.

In nature patterns are restricted, and it is amazing that the huge visual variety we see of organic forms is only a reworking of a comparatively few formal themes. It is those limitations, however, which bring a subtle harmony and beauty to the natural world.

The branching of trees for instance, is not unlike the branching of rivers seen from the air. Crystal grains are not unlike soap bubbles or the plates of a tortoise shell. Then the uncurling fiddle heads of ferns resemble spiral galaxies and water emptying down a drain.

Meandering snakes, rivers and loops of rope adopt the same pattern, as do cracking mud or the markings of a giraffe.

Taking note of topography, agricultural patterns and landforms from the air is a good way of getting the feel for any region.

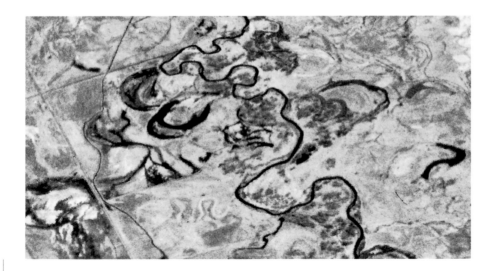

The patterns
found in nature
are often
replicated
in art and
architecture.

It almost seems that nature has her favourite patterns – spirals, meandering and branching occur again and again. The spiral is very versatile: used in replication from DNA to the arrangement of matter in a galaxy.

Three-dimensional pentagons make up most of the flower shapes, while hexagons make up most of the two-dimensional patterns but never by themselves enclose three-dimensional space.

Despite the diversity of perceived objects, if you look at the construction of matter, you will see that nature has little choice in her assignment of rules to players. For her productions are encumbered by the constraints of three-dimensional space and the necessary relations among the sizes of things, all conditioned by extreme frugality.

While pattern was used in the ancient world, there's a world of difference between pattern and decoration made up of pattern, for although all patterns are decoration, not all decorations are pattern.

Patterns may be defined as a simple decoration that is produced when a fixed shape or motif is repeated at regular intervals in a given direction. The mathematics of modular gradation is as old as time itself and has formed the basis for the design of art, architecture, music and drama. Today most aspects of contemporary experience are open to modular analysis. Computer technology is really a modular process. And modern optical instruments have enabled us to look at some of nature's patterns.

Modernism was to do with stripping away embellishment (decoration), but pure pattern still intrigues, and the rich patterning of non-European peoples has and is of an increasing interest linking pattern to regionalism. Modern technology plays its role, and you cannot ignore the hypnotic effect of identical advertising posters in the subway, houses in a development, or cars parked in a lot. They may not be decorative, but their rhythms are symbolic of our contemporary world.

Non-figurative artistic patterning was a highly developed art form of the Islamic world. Such patterning lent itself to the decoration of the portable, functional objects of a largely nomadic population. Important buildings like schools or mosques were also highly decorated – possibly as an alternative visual stimulation to the aridity of the desert.

Repeating patterns in contemporary housing has a hypnotic effect.

These patterns are constructed with the compass and straight edge. It was the first time that the circle had been used as a basis of patterning in culture, playing an important role in calligraphy, 'the geometry of the line', as well.

Islam is a totally consuming religion. Every aspect of the faithful's life is artistic expression, therefore is part of that religion; calligraphic art was used to describe the word of God, and as decoration it was a constant sign of his presence. The actual patterns expressed certain Islamic principles such as unity in multiplicity and reinforced the belief in a universe based on logic and order.

Important Islamic buildings like schools or mosques are often beautifully decorated with colourful patterns that express Islamic principles.

# PART III:
# THE ART
# OF DESIGN

# ON ART AND GARDEN DESIGN

In the late 1950s, when he began working for landscape architects Brenda Colvin and, subsequently, Sylvia Crowe, John met Susan and Geoffrey Jellicoe. She was a photographer and plantswoman; he was an architect and landscape architect who saw a connection between architecture and landscape design and between landscape design and painting. Simply put, Jellicoe, a modernist, believed that designed landscape could be considered works of art and that trends in painting led trends in landscape design. The pair took John under their wings and with them he visited art galleries and gardens. It was they who introduced him to one of John's 'heroes', Roberto Burle Marx.

John's exposure to modernist, especially abstract, art, his work at *Architectural Design* magazine and, presumably, his discussions with the Jellicoes had a profound and lasting effect on his approach to his work. For the rest of his life he visited art museums at every opportunity as he travelled the world. In 2012 the Courtauld Gallery in London held what John called 'a small, jewel-like exhibition' entitled 'Mondrian/Nicholson in Parallel'. Though he had been influenced by their paintings since the 1950s, his enthusiasm for their work was reignited. He wrote about it on his blog, 'John Brookes Rants and Raves', reminding his readers of the connection between art and the garden.

Abstract painting's emphasis on line, shape, rhythm and colour is relevant to the art of designing a garden.

## MONDRIAN AND NICHOLSON

Talk about garden or landscape design and the conversation focuses on plant material, but I would like to talk about pure design, and more specifically garden design. But when I launch into this and mention modernism in architecture or abstraction in painting as having any relevance, the eyes of my listener glaze over.

'What's that got to do with gardening?' I can hear them thinking.

Well, first of all, it has nothing to do with gardening; I am talking about the art of design.

A classic garden, we all know, has formality and symmetry in its layout (though there was a hiccup in the eighteenth century). A modern garden, which could still be formal, but because of its smaller size and the amount we require of it – a lawn, a pond, a play area, a veg plot, some herbs, a tool shed – is less likely to have symmetry in its layout.

And this distinction between the form of the design and its content was first contended by the modernist movement of the 1920s and 1930s, in which the form alone became the most important visual issue.

In the art world – and I, perhaps presumptuously, include garden design as part of it – we, its practitioners, must surely need to be aware of its movements. Impressionism we know freed colour from its traditional role of defining objects, and post-Impressionism took this further. Cubism was inspired by African art and so on. An alternative to realism was introduced in the form of abstract art where there was an emphasis on line, shape, rhythm and colour. This movement was only initially appreciated at the time by an avant-garde.

In the early 1930s the artist Ben Nicholson started visiting Paris and came to know many of the artists working with abstraction in their painting and sculpture. There he met Piet Mondrian, who in his studio had cards painted in primary colours pinned upon its plain white walls in a sort of collage. Nicholson was impressed by their calm. A friendship developed. With the increasing threat of Nazism (Mondrian was on the Nazi's list of degenerate artists), he was persuaded to move to London in 1938, and there he had a studio in Belsize Park in the garden of the house in which Nicholson worked.

Mondrian's work began to influence that of Nicholson, who himself was producing a form of abstracted painting, but which now became simpler and stronger, and was composed of interlocking or overlaying planes of much softer colour than Mondrian's primaries. Nicholson's use of tones created a two-dimensional effect, while Mondrian's cool precision was very flat.

Ultimately, Nicholson started to produce simple white painted reliefs which introduced the third dimension of height or thickness into his work, in that the play of light introduces shadow lines into the planes of his design. It is this play of shape, pattern, colour and mass which I try to introduce to my students of garden design.

Early on I started to play with regular proportions (a sort of graph paper) taken from the proportions of the house which a garden adjoins, and which got me looking at Mondrian's designs.

This progression through to Ben Nicholson' s work quite took my breath away when seen on the walls of the Courtauld Gallery, and I now see what the byline 'in parallel' meant. And I wasn't aware of their friendship.

Of course, there was a sort of dogged resentment at the time to this alternative to our established tradition of painting, rooted as it was in ruralism. The reaction was a return to a form of representationalism, and a backwards glance to the Arts and Crafts movement, perhaps understandably, as a security through the uncertainty of war years.

Not until there was a post-war calm did any modern feeling (though still with an Arts and Crafts affinity) start to get through to the establishment. It came from Scandinavia. Only with the Festival of Britain in 1951 was modernism again even contemplated by British designers, architects and the public.

For anyone interested in garden design I believe an understanding of the development of twentieth-century painting can be important, for it is a comment on society. And what society is thinking at any one time has always influenced the scale, form and content of our gardens.

John's design for the headquarters of Penguin Books was highly influenced by the paintings of Piet Mondrian.

   HOW TO DESIGN A GARDEN

In addition to Mondrian and Nicholson, John loved the connection he saw between contemporary French gardens and the later paintings of Picasso and Matisse. He devised various exercises to help his students understand the link between abstraction and garden design and to help them think about their work more conceptually.

In Russia he discovered the paintings of the avant-garde Kazimir Malevich, whose work had inspired many later abstract artists. He loved Malevich's work, which he saw first in St Petersburg. In this article for the Russian magazine *Gallery SPD*, John describes a class in which he helped his students break from conventional ideas into an entirely different way of thinking about design using Malevich's paintings as a teaching tool.

## AN INTRODUCTION TO KAZIMIR MALEVICH

For a number of years, I have been teaching students of garden and landscape design in Russia and have found that most of them seem to have little awareness of what abstraction is all about. They also have no knowledge or very little about modernism either, their design concerns being rooted (not surprisingly, I suppose), in horticultural practice, which is good, but it negates the possibilities of their experiencing wider design horizons.

This is not so different from my experience back home in Britain and elsewhere. It all depends upon from which discipline the student came to think about landscape design. Here increasingly they are coming over from architecture, for instance, from television design and other aspects of the visual arts.

Recently, at a garden and landscape design school in St Petersburg (Green Arrow), I decided to address this sad omission and to introduce my students to the designs of Kazimir Malevich. This, of course, made a change from looking at eighteenth-century coats of arms planted out in French marigolds which they could see at the Imperial Gardens festivals. At the festival there was also one lonely exhibition by Elena Markitanova of Malevich's *Two Male Figures*. It was the landscape pattern in which they stood which interested me. For ground pattern in landscape design is surely the basis on or in which we live?

I enlarged some of Malevich's designs and got my students to trace over them accurately to get their feel. It is all very well to look, but draw over and colour and you experience the patterns and their relationships. I then

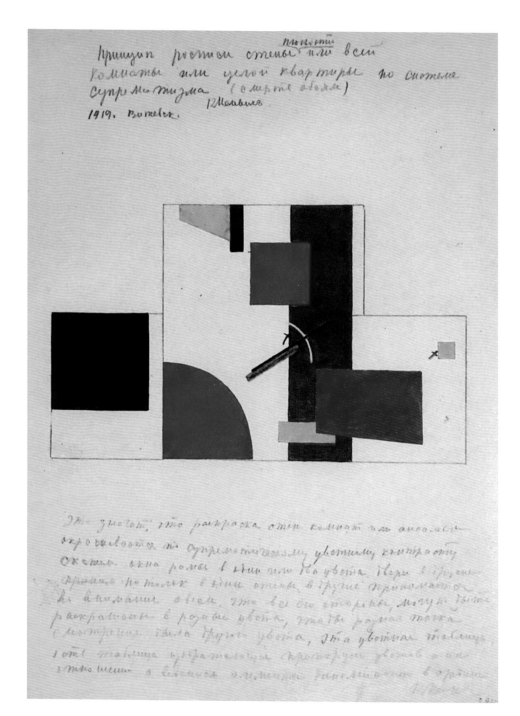

John was fascinated by the paintings of the Russian Kazimir Malevich, whose work influenced the abstract artists who followed him.

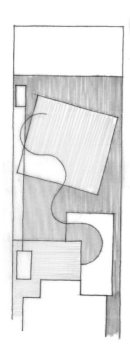

suggested that they place over their drawings the plan of a domestic structure, and to try to convert the Malevich design into a practical garden pattern (apologizing secretly to Mr M!). The house needed a drive, for instance, some water perhaps, planting which enclosed the site, and plantings which were more decorative.

The students began to think in broad masses, as in collage design, rather than their previous rather dated designs which seemed to evolve in the leftover spaces between tortuous circulatory patterns. In Britain I abuse the work of Ben Nicholson and Piet Mondrian in the same way. Malevich was much earlier!

The students produced some really interesting layouts which they had to admit had taken them into a whole new world of conceptual design. Some I suspect were reeling a bit as they left the studio – that crazy Englishman, they were thinking.

Looking at abstract paintings and creating a collage of shapes that will ultimately form a garden's design is a good way of breaking away from old design traditions and connecting a garden with contemporary architecture.

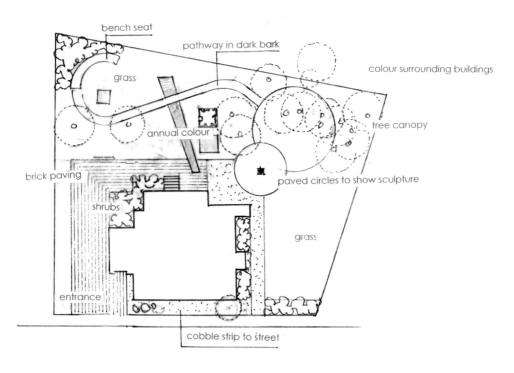

bench seat

pathway in dark bark

colour surrounding buildings

grass

annual colour

tree canopy

brick paving

paved circles to show sculpture

shrubs

grass

entrance

cobble strip to street

In 1961 Theo Crosby, an architect and sculptor, designed single-storey conference and exhibition buildings for the International Union of Architects Conference. He asked John to design the associated courtyard which featured a sculpture by the English abstract sculptor Anthony Caro. As John wrote in his autobiography, *A Landscape Legacy*, 'Theo's concept was to integrate art and architecture by using outdoor sculpture and modern interior murals and sculpture. It was very well received.'

John's preoccupation with the relationship between art and the garden and art and architecture matured in the decades following this seminal experience. His conviction that garden design was an art form was reinforced by trends and his own travels. It was also reinforced by his deepening concern about the environment and the commercialization of garden centres which, writ large, threatened to homogenize garden design.

In this thoughtful and brilliant piece written in 2002 for fellow professionals, John shows that the connection between art and garden and garden and art is multifaceted. Its commercialization, like the commercialization of horticulture, has eroded the distinctiveness of 'places' and, moreover, has led to the disconnect between humans and nature. He argues that art, particularly land art, can serve as a bridge to re-establish the bond with local vernacular and 'to win back nature as space which allows sensory perception, space in which a relationship between people and the environment becomes possible again, most importantly, at the human and wildlife level'.

In drawing a parallel between land artists and landscape and garden designers, John calls on the latter to go into their own landscapes and learn to 'look', to develop an 'eye', so that they can reinforce local distinctiveness and, in the process, reconnect with nature. John's directive about 'going into the landscape' has become more poignant in the face of the Covid-19 pandemic. During the pandemic the importance of reconnecting with nature was revealed in new ways as the outdoors became a refuge from isolation imposed by lockdowns and the fear of transmission. At the same time, the pause in human activity permitted animal activity in the natural world to increase, making us more aware of their significance. The inability to travel at will forced us into our own locales, providing an important opportunity for us to appreciate our local vernaculars, nature and landscapes in a different way, as well as an opportunity to connect with gardening and horticulture.

## LOCAL DISTINCTIVENESS AND LAND ART

I don't think that anyone has really explored the connection between garden design and land art – or rather I don't think it has been done by a garden designer. Land artists are a little superior about garden designers, but then I don't think they see us as artists. That's another story!

Before exploring what the accepted sense of land art is, I think I should discuss art in nature. And before that, something about local distinctiveness, since it is this that we should be celebrating. Over the years I have been fascinated by the work of Angela King and Sue Clifford at Common Ground and I owe much of what I write to them.*

As early as 1889, Richard Jeffries wrote in his *Field and Hedgerow* that if every plant and every flower were found in all places the charm of locality would not exist. Everything varies and that variation gives 'interest'. So much of the detail and diversity in our everyday lives and landscapes has vanished, and standardization, increased mobility, mass production, global communication, fad and fashion are all helping to further erode local differences which ought to be an enrichment to our lives.

The erosion of local differences and the bleaching of identity also apply to most worked landscapes in Europe for there is little left that is untouched. This applies to public open spaces and, of course, to private gardens. For garden centres tend to sell the same plants irrespective of local conditions. Instead of swapping plants and taking cuttings from neighbours, we are now impatient and buy more and more commercially. The long history of domestic plant cultivation passed down through generations has been broken and the stories, both personal and botanical, have become forgotten, so that plant

The flyer used by the group 'Common Ground' lays out some of the concepts at the heart of local distinctiveness.

COMMON GROUND RULES FOR LOCAL DISTINCTIVENESS

Fight for AUTHENTICITY and integrity. Keep places lived in, worked in and real.

Demand the BEST of the new.

CHANGE things for the better, not for the sake of it!

Let the CHARACTER of the people and place *express* itself. Challenge corporate identity before it kills our high streets. Give local shops precedence.

Value the COMMONPLACE. Our cultural landscapes are our *ordinary* history and *everyday* nature intertwined.

CONTINUITY show. Decay is an important process. Don't tidy things up so much that the layers of history and reclamation by nature are obliterated.

Defend DETAIL. Respond to the local and to the *vernacular*. No new building or development need be bland or brash.

*Local* DIALECT should be spoken, heard and seen.

EATING should be a *creative* act. Buy local and seasonal.

We need ENCHANTMENT, clear streams as well as clean water in our *daily* lives.

ENHANCE the natural features – rivers and brooks, hills and valleys, woods and heaths. Never let a stream be culverted, out of sight and open to abuse.

Take the place's FINGERPRINT. Forget words such as resource, site, customers and public. Abstractions lead us astray. Think and talk about places and people.

Get to know your GHOSTS. The hidden and unseen *stories and legends* are as important as the visible.

GROUND yourself. attachment is the first step to changing the world.

Don't fossilise places. HISTORY is a continuing process, not just the past. *Celebrate* time, place and the *seasons* with feasts and festivals.

Work for local IDENTITY. *Oppose* monoculture in our fields, parks, gardens and buildings. Resist formulaic designs and automatic ordering from pattern books which homogenise and deplete.

Our IMAGINATION needs diversity and *variegation*. We need standards, not standardisation.

JETTISON your car whenever you can and go by public transport. Places are for people and nature. Cars detach us from places and unwittingly cause their destruction.

Know your place. Facts and surveys are not the same as KNOWLEDGE and *wisdom*. Itinerant expertise needs to meet with aboriginal, *place-based* knowledge so that we can make the best of both worlds.

The LAND is sacred in many cultures. Why have we put a protective noose around the spectacular and the special and left the rest? *All of our surroundings* are important to someone.

* Established in 1983, Common Ground is an arts and environmental charity. Angela King served as Friends of the Earth's Wildlife Campaigner from 1971; she led the 'Save the Whale' campaign and fought to challenge the use of furs in fashion and helped to bring about the British ban on otter hunting in 1978. Sue Clifford served on Friends of the Earth's board between 1974 and 1981 and was a lecturer in rural and natural resources planning, first at the Polytechnic of Central London and then at University College London.

associations which characterize different places have become diluted, and gardens and plants become more to do with fashion and hence the time rather than place.

Wise gardeners and garden designers intuitively think about soil type, microclimate, aspect, altitude, local history, the age and style of the house, and how the garden sits in relation to it and the surrounding areas. This emphasis on place is what is so important, but individualism and free choice are being led by something of the spirit of the time and the underlying thought process of 'place' is being lost.

If you start exposing the social layers which define the concept of place, you start to think more closely of the meaning of what local distinctiveness is all about.

As we considered the garden's relationship to its land, traditionally the house, too, would have related, since it could only be built of the materials which were locally available. We call this idiom the 'vernacular'. And the same set of circumstances which produced a building vernacular also produced areas of specific husbandry – what the land could provide, such as timber, mixed arable farming, monocultures of wheat and corn or just good grazing – and so land patterns evolved through working the landscape.

The cultural landscape of a region is reflected in a variety of ways that celebrate its unique distinctiveness, and integrating that distinctiveness in a garden's design adds romance and resonance.

Then if you relate house to village and the community, you are starting to appreciate your cultural landscape. The cultural landscape may be defined by history or by location. It was and is often described by writers and poets and delineated by artists. Again, in regions where we have over hundreds of years of husbandry and cultivation, we have field names and pub names and street names, too. Add in local folk customs which have produced seasonal festivals and fairs since time immemorial. All these features celebrate the unique distinctiveness of an area, and I would suggest they can provide a resonance and a romance to our garden design work. And into this rich tapestry of community we add our landscape pattern as well.

For the designer an interest may be of land pattern by a particular type of cultivation or natural growth. Individual plants relate to particular areas in Mediterranean regions: for instance, we all know the olive tree, cypress and grape vine. But the varieties alter according to soil and situation, household usage, even from valley to valley, and so the food and produce vary too, for the distance we could travel 100 years ago was defined by how far a horse could go and back by nightfall.

To a degree you can read the distinctiveness of an area from a topographical survey, its levels, streams and rivers, shoreline, field patterns and tree felling. As farm becomes village, each will have a name that might tell you of the site, its people and its social hierarchy. Fly over the landscape and your survey really comes alive for under the agricultural field patterns you can see past river courses, past buildings, even signs of past cultures and civilizations.

Local distinctiveness in some areas is being celebrated in a number of ways; people are becoming increasingly more interested in sustaining local nature rather than subduing it. Gardens, of course, can help create an understanding of growing plants and help people to see the sense of welcoming nature into their lives. If the gardener cannot see the sense of building a sensitive relationship with nature, how can one expect others who do not delve in the soil to do so?

Sympathetic gardening implies putting less effort in to get more out, letting go of neatness, and watching nature develop a theme and redefining the word 'weed'. The garden pest is the conservationist's life blood.

As in private gardens so in public or municipal spaces, there is huge scope to encourage people to become more aware of what gives places identity: what makes them different from each other as well as what they share.

A major issue of our age, however, is an increasingly disturbed relationship between nature and humanity and the ensuing worldwide threat to ecological balance. We seem still to be seeking a technological solution to a crisis often generated by technology itself. The realization that the crisis facing the environment is being caused by humans having lost their sense of place is only gradually gaining acceptance.

There is a need for a new design language which creates a far greater public discussion on this changing perception of nature. This is where landscape design can take part in creating a modern form of expression – having moved away from the classical vocabulary of 'garden art'. Once respected as an important and influential art form, this has now become hijacked by economics, manipulated by the garden centre culture, and has lost that basic correctness outlined in an awareness of what local identity was all about.

Throughout the second half of the twentieth century, the functional, the sociological and the ecological became more important than any artistic concept of what nature was about. It's that technology thing again. The search for a way out of the crisis and the increasing rejection of a purely technologically driven approach to nature can lead to a reinstatement of garden art as a unique tool of non-verbal communication and the creation of a sense of place. This, I believe, is where land art comes in as a way to win back nature as space which allows sensory perception, space in which a relationship between people and the environment becomes possible again, most importantly at the human and wildlife level. We are all of nature. The Romantic appreciation of untouched natural beauty gave way to an unrelenting harnessing of nature as a source of raw materials long ago. Now a new definition might see nature as based on a moral philosophy which values diversity, respects difference and is able to come to terms with discontinuity. Such a concept accepts that being a living organism, humans are part of nature, but as rational beings they are also able to make their own decisions and hence must accept full responsibility for their actions.

Before considering pure land art, I think we should look at art in nature, of which, as landscape designers, you should be aware.

To experience art in nature you have to get out and into nature and learn to look. Start walking and noting. If you do not sketch or photograph already, start to do so. The technological complexity of your camera does not matter. For you need to develop an eye for what you see, and then an eye for selecting the essence of it, to interpret it through the eye of your camera – of whatever type. Your project might be: 'today I want to record the feel of this place' – flat, watery, mountainous, whatever. Is it hot or cold? Is there a wind? Now the building materials (and concrete block is just fine): what is the road or path made of? Are there any fences – and, if so, what are they enclosing? Is it spring or winter or summer? This has nothing of old-world charm about it – it's pure factual observation by a sensitive eye. Now look at the earth and the plant material growing on it: what is native, what is introduced? Is there any farmed or man-made pattern?

Has your landscape any historical content or social relevance? Try digging – not literally – just a little deeper by talking to someone who lives there.

Observe and even record local materials, how they are used, why they are used, to get a sense of the local vernacular.

Developing an 'eye' requires taking the time to observe local agricultural patterns as well as the natural lie of the land and other unique details in a landscape.

You are really getting into the essence of your place but are trying to record some of this in the camera. And eventually into this you might be asked to create a landscape or garden. Will your research make any difference? It must, no matter the house design or clients for whom you work. You work with yourself long after these clients have gone. And that is what is important. We need to be land artists in our own right.

I am about to restate the obvious in talking about the materials with which you will see art in nature created.

Earth – think about it: it is not coincidental that the substance and the place have the same name. Earthworks are important in the work of artists like Sir Richard Long and Maya Lin.

Stone – along with stone, blood and bone are the most important materials worked by humans and as such has always played a pivotal role in art. Every unworked piece of stone tells a piece of landscape history through its location, type and form and is linked to its place. It often has deep relevance to past cultural histories.

Wood – used as fuel and as building material, wood is fundamental to existence and can be worked in three ways: carving, construction (beam and plank) and in its natural form as tree, trunk or branch. Wood is most dynamic in its growing form when it develops a momentum of its own and actively alters its environment. Humans have traditionally used gardening wherever it was a question of controlling this natural process of change.

There is no 'growing act' in the art world – however, many environmental artists see woody material as a metaphor for life, growth and decay, an essential part of nature and progress.

So, the natural materials of art in nature are those of the land artist as well. They are incidentally, if you hadn't realized, the basic materials with which we landscape designers work, but we too often deny the context of their origin, in the new context to which we introduce them.

'Land Art' is a name given to a movement which emerged in the United States in the 1960s in which landscape and the work of art are linked. Sculptures are not placed in the landscape; rather the landscape is the means of their creation. The artist uses earth, stone, water and other natural materials to mark, shape and build, to change and restructure landscape space with a sensitivity and a care arising from an awareness of ecological responsibility in a plastic-weary society. Land art is therefore of the land itself – it is not just using landscape as a setting. The term 'earth work' is also used.

Surely much of this description is what we are about as garden designers as well? I have a growing disquiet that in our quest for newness and originality, we are losing touch with the earth which should anchor us to it. Perhaps increasing urbanity creates a belief that we can live without nature, although at the first sign of sun in spring everybody's out in it. But we need to instil a deeper awareness in people of our earthbound being. To this end new landscapes, new

Land artists often use materials that are not intended to last but become part of the natural process of decay and renewal.

landforms, earth work or land art can, I believe, explain and enlighten us as to our own personal distinctiveness in whatever location we might be.

I believe a lot of young designers are confused with this, which I choose to call 'design philosophy', with lessons in modernism or in minimalism. How, they ask, does it all hang together? I don't think that it does necessarily. Design rules rooted in modernism are sound and sensible, but these can be overlaid with other thoughts: on styling, for instance, in planting and in choice of materials. It is when thinking of suitability to site that we might remember local distinctiveness, and it is when considering maintenance and sustainability that you might remember the landscape as it was.

Anthony Goldsworthy's use of materials varies tremendously, exploiting transitory and fragile elements that are affected by different seasons, in this instance especially by snow and ice in winter.

# ON HOW TO DESIGN

In this 2002 lecture John encourages his students to forget about plants for a while and instead to learn the language of design. He emphasizes the importance of 'developing an eye'. This, he explains, is done by learning to 'look' and, taking it a step further, to analyse what one sees. He adds that it is important to visit art galleries and study forms and shapes to understand how to apply them – and practicality – to a garden's layout. The other essential skill for a designer, he concludes, is how to produce technical drawings. He steadfastly believed that designers should draw their plans by hand rather than relying on computer programmes because he thought the link between what the eye saw and the hand drew enriched the design process.

Just as learning to 'look' at the landscape is essential to developing an 'eye', so is going to art galleries and studying shapes, as in this collage by Ben Nicholson.

## LEARNING TO LANDSCAPE AND THE ART OF DESIGN

'Gardens are for people,' to quote Thomas Church.

Increasingly, we are concerned with gardens in a natural setting, and it is the analysis of that setting which sets the scene for the garden's subsequent development.

I want to talk about learning to landscape and to try to give you some insight into the art of garden design. Note that I say the *art* of garden design – which initially has little to do with the craft of gardening.

And that really is the first hurdle which so many potential garden designers have to get over – forget about plants (for a while). We are seeking to produce a working layout for a family in the space around their home. It might include a huge list of wants from the usual kids' play space to growing vegetables, screening the pool, installing a jacuzzi, hiding the caravan, and a place for logs, the compost pile, a greenhouse and so on. The latest request I had in the States besides the BBQ (on which you could cook an ox) was for a pizza oven. We are furnishing a room outside, in fact.

Now add to all this the orientation of the site, its location, the climate, the soil (or lack of it), global warming, horticultural knowledge and the inevitable low maintenance requirement. You have quite a complex conundrum to resolve.

Oh yes, one other thing: it all has to be done as cheaply as possible, said by the client in all seriousness, when you can see his and hers BMWs in the garage, you've had coffee in a brand new kitchen, and that photo with the palm trees looks remarkably like a second home somewhere.

So, the garden designer has to be a businessperson, a diplomat and a magician.

Actually, I've laid it on with a trowel. The diversity of the job is what makes it so interesting.

What is essential when starting out to learn to do the job professionally is to learn the language of design, which comes through learning how to look. This is something to do with 'having an eye', we would say, as well as learning to analyse what you see.

Developing an eye comes through going to art galleries and looking at forms and shapes, both realistic and abstract. It's to do with composing a picture if you are a photographer. The best camera in the world can't give you an eye. It's the same with sketching – what you leave out is as important as what you put in (think of Chinese or Japanese art). The shapes of a garden, and its masses and voids, create the 'wow' factor. This is another important element you need to learn to analyse.

The other basic for a garden designer is learning how to produce a technical drawing – a plan in fact – learning how to measure up and then scale down to plan size. 'Oh! that's maths,' some will wail. Actually, it's easy but years of prejudice sometimes have to be tackled. If you set aside those prejudices, I believe that anyone can draw, as we prove time and again on our courses. Yes, some will do it better than others, but it's the content of the drawing that is important, not its rendering.

So, how do we start to design a garden?

The first steps in designing a garden, whether your own or one for a client, always involve the most fundamental, sometimes the most tedious, part of the process. John believed that these initials stages were vital to the planning and ultimate execution of a plan, whether done all at once or in stages over a period of time. I recall taking his masterclass at the New York Botanical Garden where my brain was seared with his admonishment that 'if job is worth doing at all – it is worth doing well,' a quote he attributed to his father.

This is his introductory lecture about the very basic process of creating the essential site plan and site assessment, and it is as relevant to the budding designer as to the aspiring homeowner. From survey to site assessment to initial thoughts about layout, John reminds his students that the practicalities of storage, drainage and fixed elements like manholes all need thought. He also highlights the importance of getting a feel not just for the site but for its surroundings as well right from the very beginning of the process.

Creating a beautiful garden requires tedious but essential first steps like measuring and assessing a site.

## FIRST STEPS TO DESIGNING YOUR GARDEN

The permutations and possibilities of gardens are endless and vary in scale from the urban courtyard to the suburban plot and right through to the country garden.

The common denominator of all these garden possibilities are the people who use them. It is not the plants which grow in them since they vary so much whether in a warm climate or a cold one.

But people and their needs do not vary so much, though their use of the garden will change in the different seasons. Children will still play out there and gardeners will garden when they can. Some garden space will be required for storage — for cycles, tools, the mower — and for rubbish cans and then the compost heap. And there may be a fuel store, an oil tank, a greenhouse, perhaps, or some cold frames.

In warmer climates or seasons just sitting about in sun or shade is therapeutic. The meal or a drink outside in the evening, after a day in the city, is really revitalizing.

The common denominator in garden design is people and how they use their gardens.

Even for those living in a colder climate when the garden is not such an inviting place, there are still jobs to be done and access is necessary. And, one doesn't stop looking out of the window, so your view is important. This can often be improved by the use of the right plant material, but the decorative elements of that space — that is, the plants — come later in the design process.

The concept of having a garden is pretty exciting, particularly if you have small children, because they can be out there quite a lot of their time. In larger gardens they can set up a tent and camp, or where there are larger trees, they make swings, even tree houses.

But for others — it's a place of your own outside in which to be quiet, sunbathe or eat out in summer. With busy lifestyles for many the idea of the garden as a retreat in the evening and at weekends is more and more appealing.

It's a place to have a pond or some water, which provides endless enjoyment and interest. Not only in the fish and water plants, but the insects which the water brings and the birds which come to drink and feed.

The garden is also a place to grow herbs and a few vegetables as well.

Determining what needs a garden has to serve is another basic first step.

So, a garden is different things to different people. Its possibilities seem endless, though space must be a limiting factor as is, of course, the time required for its maintenance. Like a small kitchen, a small garden needs careful organizing, but what comes out of it and the enjoyment from it can amaze you and your friends.

## THINKING AHEAD

I would like to help you think ahead to what you really need out there. Eliminate the fantasies and begin to organize that space so that it becomes the garden which you envisaged.

For example, a small town garden might start as a bare space, but by using areas of brick paving to match the house, the design will connect the two. With a bit of height and ultimately with plants you can create something really special.

But before you go to mad thinking about lawn and roses, let's get the whole design sorted first.

What is really important are the proportions of a garden. The spaces need to be simple and generous (scaled up or down according to its overall size): the terrace, the plantings, the grass area and so on. Too often the gardener gets carried away with detail, which fusses and clutters the overall effect.

## THE FIRST EXPLORATORY STEPS

There is no way around it; I am going to have to talk 'design' for a moment. Let's not confuse a conversation about design with a conversation about plants

or their maintenance. This is just about shape initially as we look at the garden two-dimensionally on paper: its length and its breadth. And some thoughts about height, the third dimension, and with that you start to provide enclosure. For height may just be a step, a retaining wall, some shrubs or a tree.

In garden design, unlike other areas of design, we have a fourth dimension – time – in that living things grow, so what starts out small can end up large. But that all comes with right plant, right place.

MAKE A SURVEY

In the same way as it is wise to know the measurements of your room before you go out and buy a new table (to ensure that it fits), it makes sense to have an accurate survey of your garden as well. If you think that sounds too technical, what I mean is 'go and measure it up!' If it is just a rectangular plot, it is easy. But if the shape is irregular or has odd levels, it can be more difficult. When your site is too tricky to measure up simply, because it is overgrown or there are changes of level, you can ask a surveyor to do the job for you so it will really be accurate.

In some countries the deeds to your house will probably contain an outline of the site, but it may only be that, with no detail. That plan can be enlarged at a print shop so you can then mark on it the existing features around which your ultimate plan will work.

To make a simple survey of your garden, suppose it is more or less flat and first of all sketch the outline of the house in the middle of a sheet of blank paper.

If you use graph paper and know the size and scale of each square it might be easier – one square represents one square metre or it might represent one square foot.

When you plot the house put in the ground-floor doors and windows by taking running measurements with your tape along its frontage. I use a big tape measure, the one you wind up, which usually is 30 m/100 ft long.

If the site isn't absolutely square or rectangular, take more than one offset to get the correct angle of the boundary line. To do this, take a boundary measurement off one corner of the house. And then take another measurement from the corner to a tree or some other fixed feature. This is called triangulation and will help you get the correct angles of the boundary line.

But if you are feeling a bit lazy about this (and let's face it, the odd small measurement which is not absolutely accurate doesn't affect initial planning), lay out the tape on the ground and pace by the side of it to gauge your pace length and just use that technique to measure up your offsets.

Once you have established the offset measurements, plot them on to your paper plan, to the same scale, and you will establish where your boundary lies in relation to your house. Repeat the process to establish where there are any fixed features in the garden – a tree trunk, perhaps, or a manhole cover – they are always in the way.

I do not want to make too heavy weather of this survey business, though it is necessary to cover as many eventualities and permutations as possible right from the start. And as my father would have said, 'If job is worth doing at all – it is worth doing well.'

Now, just sit down on the step to the sliding door, look out of the kitchen window, or hang out of your bedroom window if it looks down on your garden, and have beautiful thoughts – but think of them in the light of what exists out there. During the measuring up process you often discover much more about the site. What about the views out – good or bad? Which side faces south? Or, where is the sun at noon (it will be lower in the winter, of course) because the direction of the sun – and depending whether you like

A site assessment should be to scale and have a catalogue of the site's characteristics but does not have to be a work of art.

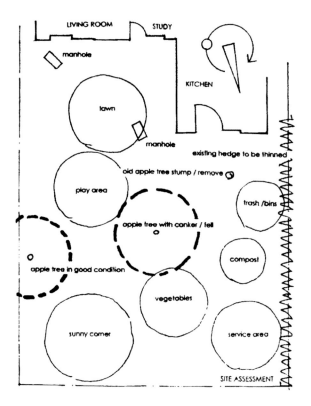

LIVING ROOM        STUDY

manhole

KITCHEN

lawn

manhole

existing hedge to be thinned

old apple tree stump / remove

play area

trash /bins

apple tree with canker / fell

compost

apple tree in good condition

vegetables

sunny corner

service area

SITE ASSESSMENT

HOW TO DESIGN A GARDEN

sun or shade – will dictate your terrace position, where the vegetable plot should be and so on.

And what of other drain or power line runs? Whether thinking about town, suburban and even country gardens, you must discover where the services run in from the street.

SITE ASSESSMENT

Put all this information on to your plan. This is now your site assessment. And the final part of your site assessment is to put a name to what is growing out there. If it's a tree put in the spread of its head, not only its trunk. As you measure up, think about sitting in its summer shade, cool drink in hand. That should really get you going!

Garden designers, or a homeowner who doesn't live on the site, should take photos of the site so you can carry on thinking about what you want when you are back home or in your studio. While there I always try to decide on the 'feel' of the garden I want to create – it is to do with the 'feel' of the house and the client – will it be wilder, will water come into the picture?

If you are not living on site, it is very helpful to take numerous photos from different angles to remind you of details that might be forgotten or overlooked.

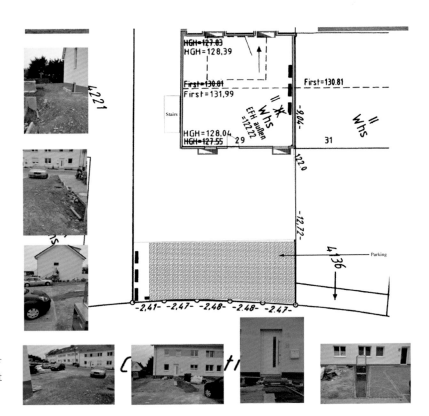

## MAJOR WORKS

For those lucky enough to be building their house it is often necessary at a very early stage – even before the house is built – to consider where something as major as a swimming pool will be located. Ha! my readers in cooler climates think – lucky indeed – but if you live nearer the equator a swimming pool can be a necessity not only because of the summer heat, but often to occupy children during long summer holidays. The pool becomes a vital focus to family living. With it goes, however, the inevitable need to locate pool plant, equipment and toy storage, and eventually saunas, barbeques, pizza ovens. Also, safety fences (a legal necessity in many places) and access from outside (for maintenance and visitors to the pool) need to be planned – it's all quite a performance.

I have not yet mentioned a site with level differences. They can be tricky to manage because where you alter them innocently you also alter the drainage, which can affect not only your house in extreme cases, but more often water availability to any existing vegetation, let alone the removal of topsoil.

I would always advise taking professional advice where you are considering moving soil around or creating retaining walls which are over 1 m/39 inches high. The odd step or low wall is fine, but you need to know what you are digging into. In colder climates, footings become essential so you should know the recommended depth of a footing for any retaining walls or steps.

Which, of course, brings me to the consideration of the soil in your garden. The welfare of your soil – and what you can grow in what you have got – needs a chapter of its own. Its types and properties are so varied. But if you know your plants, you can get a pretty good idea of your soil both from what is growing naturally and what neighbours might have in their garden.

## THINKING ABOUT LAYOUT

Let us go back to thinking about the layout, whether an empty new site, overgrown or just the previous owner's mess!

So where to start? It is important not to rush into anything, and a good plan with forward thinking makes sense. Remember that if you are starting a new garden (with often a new home and all its expenses) it isn't built overnight. It might be phased in steps over a period of time but get those steps right. It's planning again! First, to get the feel for what will be your garden and its setting, go for an exploratory walk round the neighbourhood; see what is growing, and ask neighbours about the wind, the soil and how much rain you might expect.

The primary necessity, particularly on sites with difficult access, is to get excess soil and rubbish removed before your house and garden building obstructs access, though this can be an expensive operation. In this garden, the excess soil from digging the pond was used to create mounds that provided privacy for this Russian cottage.

When John was working at *Architectural Design* magazine in the early 1960s, he was initially tasked with redrawing architects' plans for publishing. Immersed in the most avant-garde architecture, he developed a strong understanding of what he called 'the module' on which modern architecture was based. It was from this experience that he developed his grid method of design. This method, he said, imposed discipline on his own designs and helped him create a proportional relationship between a garden and the structure it surrounded (or that surrounded it). As he wrote in his memoir, *A Landscape Legacy*, 'From the grid geometric curves and squares could be introduced to create that simple flowing line, defining clear spaces.' The geometry and flowing lines were then translated into the elements of the garden, from terraces to play areas to pools to service areas.

The grid method is not to be confused with a chequerboard pattern, which John often used in his designs to break up larger areas of tarmac or paving. It is instead a tool or template that is binned after it is no longer needed, though the chequerboard pattern it suggests might be incorporated in a design.

This lecture introduces the beginning designer or homeowner to the grid method, and thus offers the necessary tools to create a garden design that is linked to the building it surrounds through proportion and alignment – in the context of the demands and potential of the site and the fourth dimension of time.

Think of the garden as an extension of your home. The garden is for people – though furnished with plants.

## THINKING ABOUT WHAT YOU WANT AND THE GRID

I want to talk to you now about deciding what you want out there and creating your own system as a basis in which to work using the grid principle.

Do try to be realistic in your aspirations for the garden: think about its construction, who will do the work and, almost more importantly, who will maintain and look after the garden when it is completed.

Building a garden is not a cheap operation, but I believe that it is worth doing well. That means making sure, for example, that paths, steps and terraces are built on a sound foundation, and any sort of water has a safety factor built in – those sort of things.

One of the aspects that I think confuses people is imagining their garden, whatever its size, as a place for plants alone. It most definitely is not.

Smaller spaces, in particular, should be thought about as more of a home extension – a room outside (sound familiar?). For as well as this room being furnished with plants, it is also a place, for example, for children to play. Plants might be restricted to pots which are tough and can take a few hard knocks from kids' play.

And it's a place to have meals outside and to take the sun. Grass may not be necessary but a good working surface is, for tricycles, bikes and balls, for dining tables and chairs, for recliners and even sculpture.

In larger gardens you can start to think about things more horticulturally, though without forgetting the user element of it all. So, the garden is for people – though furnished with plants.

### MAKE A LIST

Start to list what you want. And if you are one of a couple, both of you have your say and battle out between you what is practical. As a garden designer I often feel that my job is as a sort of referee!

When you have decided what you want (and what you can afford), start to position your functions on your plan. You will find that the practicalities of the site will probably start to dictate what should go where. Refer back to your site assessment.

Start with major items such as a swimming pool or additional parking and work down to a summer house or storage building. Some structures are nice to look at, others are not. One person needs the sun, perhaps, and the other doesn't. Then I think, what about a vegetable patch and a space for herbs near the storage with a path to it? Perhaps you want some paving and a pond, and do you want a paved terrace near the summer house? Existing vegetation or trees will often help define these positions, as will any views out of the garden, but be aware that views looking out often allow winds to blow in.

'I just want a place for the kids to play,' you bleat. Fine! Grass it all with planting round but remember the mowing!

'Oh!' you say, 'I don't want maintenance.' Well, you can always tarmac over the garden, I reply in desperation or, as was the trend at one time, cover it in decking.

The word garden seems to conjure up plants and greenery, and for the urban resident I think this is really important, even if only to look at.

If you really are stuck for ideas, there are masses of books which you can peruse for gardens of every size and in almost every climate.

Once you have decided what you want, and where it should go, how do you go about putting it all together to make a coherent design? This is the bit that sometimes frightens people.

## WHAT SORT OF DESIGN?

It really depends upon your personal style. Making decisions about your own garden is hard. And, as a designer, I can often tell the owners' style from the inside of their houses. It's an assessment I make all the time with clients, and it often depends upon what they do for a living. An accountant will probably want a tidy garden, traditional in feel, while an architect may be prepared to 'have a go' at something more adventurous.

The building may or may not point the way to a more adventurous solution of the garden plan. Modern buildings tend to have large areas of glass which

The type of garden you choose to create depends on your style.

demand either a view into the garden alone or a more distant outlook, in which case the garden design should not get in the way.

A really arty person might want a wild garden. Controlled wildness is quite difficult to achieve, uncontrolled is no problem, and the dividing line is very fine! The wilder look tends to rely on the gardener having a good knowledge of plant material or it may get out of hand.

A fairly basic decision is whether you want to have a formal garden or a looser informal one. The strict symmetrical formal layout only works, I believe, where the garden adjoins a formal sort of house, with the door in the middle and windows which are equivalent on either side and above it.

Of course, you can have an informal garden planted in the cottagey way, but it will still need to be practical and useable, with dry paths for winter access to fuel, for instance. And a way to the vegetable plot: a must in such a garden.

There is also an intermediate style in which you create an asymmetrical layout that is formally edged, possibly with box or lavender, and infilled with looser, wilder or more cottagey planting. I think this sort of layout can fit in anywhere.

If this is too confusing let me explain a system which I think will help you. Design concepts are a nightmare to explain and understand. I have a technique for whatever your ultimate style may be and it gets the creative juices flowing! It's called the grid system.

## THE GRID SYSTEM

Over your accurate garden plan where you have designated various functions, lay a piece of tracing paper and stick it down with tape so it can't shift. Now look closely at the plan of the house and the side of it you want to work with to see if there are any regular dimensions between, say, the boundary to the corner of the house and then along the house facade. You will often find a numerical rhythm in their dimensions, such as 0, 4, 8, 12, 16. This comes about in modern building technique particularly, because doors and windows are produced to a standard size.

In older properties where this unity is not obvious, use a major element such as a double door as the figure on which you concentrate your grid. With other properties bits project and recede and these provide the rhythm. A conservatory or a bay window is often the key to it all, being the largest visible element, so work with its dimension.

My first line in drawing the grid for this house would have been down the side of the extension. The second line would have been along the extension itself parallel to the recessed part of the house. I would then halve that line, which gives me the overall grid size.

A bit of trial and error might be necessary, but because most modern houses have been built on a grid (look at an architect's plan) we can usually plug into this.

A prominent feature of the house should be used to determine the proportions of the grid and, in turn, the proportions of the garden's features.

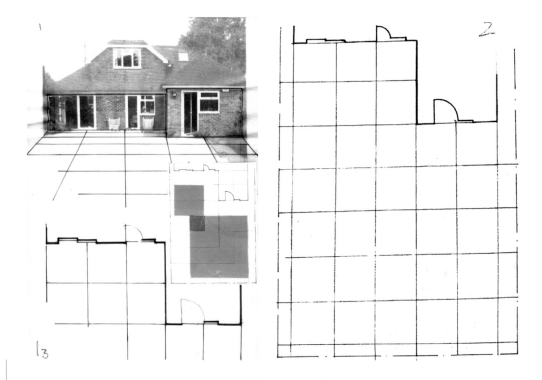

When you have worked this one out – and it will often be obvious from having taken site measurements previously – draw lines at 90 degrees to the house at each of your dimensions: they must be equal. Then draw lines parallel to the house across your initial one from the house to create a grid or graph paper for yourself. It is unique to the property; every grid is, therefore, unique to the building and site.

You will find that there are leftover bits of your grid at the edge of the site, but don't worry about them. And when designing larger, probably country gardens, you can double the size of the grid as you move away from the house. Your subsequent pattern in the enlarged grid will be more in scale with your view, the height of surrounding woodland and so on.

By the same token as you work in the area adjacent to the house, where you will want smaller areas to plant, pave or water, you can halve the grid size.

Grid proportions will always be square and should not be rounded up to the nearest metre or foot. These proportions will be approximately 1–2 m/39–84 inches in size, when close to the building, and they act as a guide to the scale of the shapes which you ultimately put into them. A garden path, for instance, may come out of a 1-metre grid, which is a good guide for the width of a small garden path.

The grid can be used to break up areas of tarmac with a pattern in granite setts or another material.

Always design from the house outwards into the garden, never from the boundary enclosure inwards. The journey starts and ends at the house – so it is here you start, as I have shown. The house is generally the biggest and therefore the most dominant element of the garden, and it should blend seamlessly into its space, whether in an urban or rural context.

Do not let the grid become a straitjacket. It is intended to get your eye used to a system of proportions.

In the third lecture of the four-part design class, John gives a bit of design theory about flow before launching into creating a design using patterns based on the grid. Think back to his exercise for his Russian students who were first told to trace a Malevich design before trying to translate it into a garden design (pp. 87–9) and John's notes on pattern (pp. 78–81). At this stage of a design an understanding of patterns in painting as well as the landscape, nature and in a garden setting becomes essential. It is the stage at which the components of a garden design become two-dimensional shapes on plan based on the grid, which ensures they are proportional and relate to the elements and style of the house.

Here John explains how to start playing with patterns in the context of a base garden plan, which he likens to a picture frame. He also introduces the 'rule of thirds'.

## SOME DESIGN THEORY

In my last talk I showed you how to create a grid system as a basis on which to design.

You should now have three layers of drawings, with your site survey on the bottom, over that your site assessment with what ideally goes where, and, finally, your grid system drawing. At long last, you can now start making patterns which you turn into a garden plan by placing on top of these layers a piece of tracing paper. All the information you need to evolve your plan should be in the three initial drawings.

On the fourth layer, start to think about combining the squares of your grid into areas. These areas can become lawn, terrace, pool or vegetable plot, and they will all have some proportional relationship back to the house and to each other.

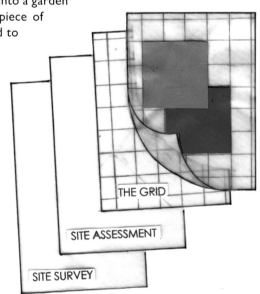

THE GRID

SITE ASSESSMENT

SITE SURVEY

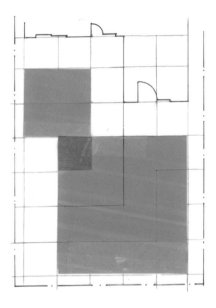

You can ring the changes with circles within the squares, or link one pattern type to another.

And as long as you take your proportions from the grid, you can move the pattern; its proportions will still be the same.

Try various patterns to encompass the functions you want of your space to get the hang of this technique and you will find that you are having fun.

## A FORMAL DESIGN

In a garden where the line of site from the door of the house divides the garden into two areas, a more formal style of design is created. Such a plan is fine for a period style property but looks heavy and out-of-date with many of today's modern homes.

And dividing a long thin garden down the middle is a recipe for disaster as it creates two even thinner spaces that are almost unusable.

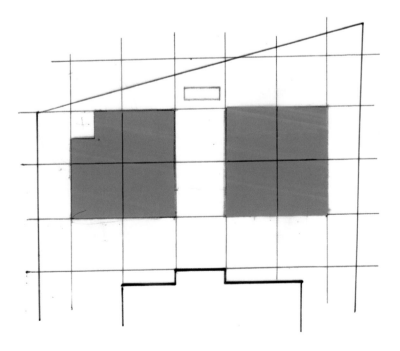

## ANTICLOCKWISE DESIGN

A garden needs both a visual and practical/physical direction of flow, but unlike the more formal period style described, which holds the central ground, the contemporary garden tends to have a clockwise or anticlockwise direction of flow round its site.

By creating more emphasis on one side of the house, perhaps a terrace, you subliminally infer a direction of flow. A terrace positioned to the right of the house gives greater emphasis to this side of the plan and the visual if not physical journey commences from right to left, giving an anticlockwise direction of flow.

## CLOCKWISE DESIGN

You could reverse the flow by placing the terrace on the opposite side. This now suggests a clockwise direction of flow and allows the designer to encourage the homeowner to explore different garden spaces.

Your choice of design direction will be influenced by lots of factors, not least personal choice. It might be that the dining terrace gets evening sun in a particular area, or it could be that the doors to the garden are on a particular side of the house. You may find that existing features such as a tree tend to

A well-designed modern garden is one in which you can control the direction which the eye takes, and which then leads the user when leaving the house. So, the plan evolves from the house which you try to link to the functions of the garden. With the help of the grid, a modern design relies on the strength of the ground pattern to delineate its functions and/or route round it.

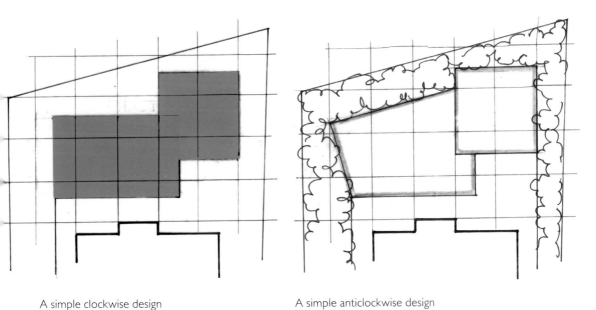

A simple clockwise design                    A simple anticlockwise design

make you walk round the garden in a certain way – well, so be it, and let this feature guide you in your patterning.

STARTING THE DESIGN
Having created your grid and understood about movement in design, it is time to think more about the design for your site. I want you to think at this stage about pattern, though, rather than garden.

This may be difficult but imagine your garden boundary as a picture frame: the house within it will be your first shape. We will call this the base shape.

Now create a simple collage of overlapping shapes, starting with your base shape, inside your picture frame. Make sure that you always leave a space between your pattern and the frame's edge, however, as this will eventually become your planting area.

You can do this by either drawing the shapes on tracing paper (it will be your fourth layer) or try cutting out several pieces of card, using the grid as a guide to their scale. You can use full grid squares or multiples, or half-grid squares, but nothing in between. Generally, stick to one sort of pattern: for instance, interlocking squares parallel with the house for a conventional approach, or turned at an angle. Eventually, you can introduce circles, even hexagonal shapes, taken perhaps from the line of a bay window or conservatory extension.

If you are working on tracing paper, lay one pattern on another, and perhaps colour some of them, or use cut-out pieces of card – it may or may not work

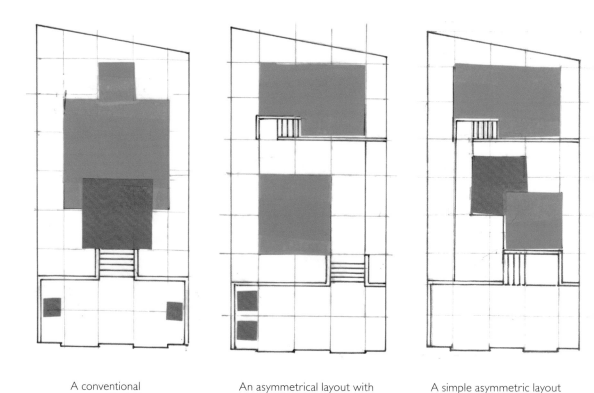

A conventional
symmetric design

An asymmetrical layout with
an anticlockwise movement

A simple asymmetric layout
with a clockwise movement

as a garden plan – but you are learning about lines and patterns along the way.
The result will eventually be so much more exciting than making a wiggly line
with a hosepipe.

PATTERN MAKING

One of the rules of this pattern making is to make sure that every shape you
use overlaps with the next. The amount of overlap is also important. You want
to establish 'strong bonds' as these patterns subliminally focus your view and
guide you round the garden when it is built.

Imagine trying to glue your pieces of card together (if that is what you are
using). A strong bond will be when two cards overlap enough to create a large
enough glueing area. Too little overlap and there will not be enough glue to
hold them and this will result in a weak and unsatisfying bond.

Circles are quite difficult to use in small spaces as, if they are too large, they
can get too close to the 'picture frame' – leading to tiny, thin planting areas that
do little for a garden.

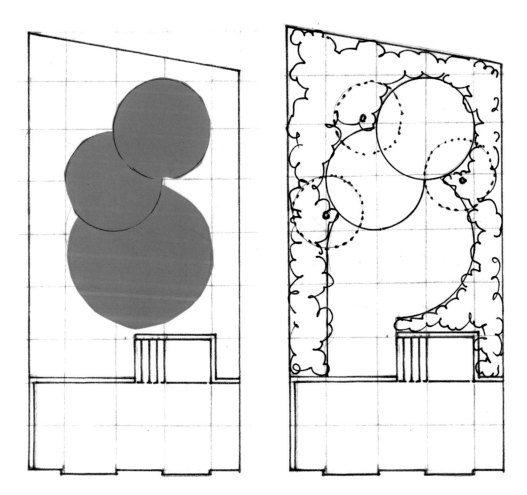

Keep a circular
pattern simple.

1 If you use circles make sure that their diameter is based on the grid square proportions.

2 Make sure they have a good strong bond.

3 Avoid nasty pointy triangular shapes, which can so easily appear but which look horrible as either paving or planting.

I would recommend avoiding circles in small urban gardens as they are likely to cause you problems. But time after time clients tell me that they don't want straight lines; curves, they say, are softer and look more natural. (Curves are more realistic, though still within the basic grid technique, within larger garden layouts. And the further you work away from the house, the more it is necessary to take on board the feeling of the garden surround.)

However, planning a garden is much the same as planning the interior of a house. You don't put an amoebic shaped carpet into a rectangular shaped

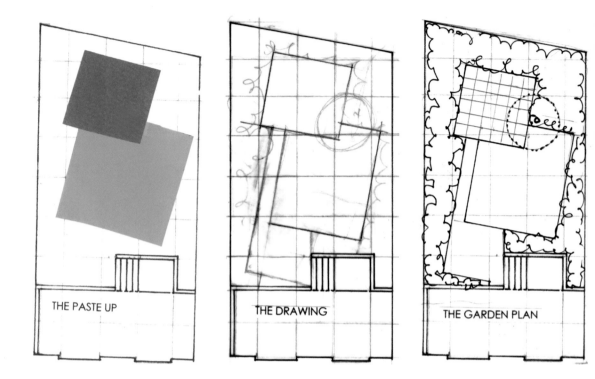

| THE PASTE UP | THE DRAWING | THE GARDEN PLAN |

room. So why put an amoebic shaped lawn into a rectangular garden? It's the furnishings which soften a room and it's the same again outside. While your plan may look hard and architectural on paper, add the differing shapes and texture of paving, water and above all plants, and they soften the layout and make it look far more natural.

You can see here the evolution from pattern to a garden plan.

You can alter the angle of your pattern, taking the shapes off the original grid. In the diagram above, the design is still clockwise in its directional flow; however, the space between the picture frame and the shapes has changed slightly, which has allowed for a more dynamic planting that is narrower in some places and wider in others. In the next two diagrams you can see a basic pattern can then be interpreted into a garden plan by defining the four basic surface treatments – that of planting, grass, paving and water (where required).

## RULE OF THIRDS

Probably the most important design rule of all I would describe as the 'rule of thirds'. Not only does it explain what shapes to use where, but also which materials are the most appropriate in different areas of the garden. Close to the house, the much-used area, hard materials should be employed to echo and complement the structure. There will be a degree of formality as well with geometric shapes as an appendix to the house shape.

In the middle third you move away from hard materials to more cut lawn, or perhaps from concrete or stone paving and paths to shingle or gravel (though well laid so that it is hard, not crunchy).

And finally, in larger gardens, move from mown lawns to rough grass, with mown paths through it, from a formal pool (used nearer the house) to a natural pond, and so to the influence of the countryside beyond – should you be lucky enough.

Obviously, great sweeping curves fit into a gentle pastoral setting; in a more angular mountain region your pattern will alter accordingly. Very flat landscapes call for simple formality.

Eventually, your planting will follow similar rules. Close to the house, often the most sheltered area, you will have more special horticultural varieties to those used to create screening and shelter at a distance away from it, until in the last third the planting can become more natural where native species and wildflowers are more appropriate.

The 'rule of thirds' provides a guide for choosing materials and how to progress from formal areas near the house to less formal areas further away.

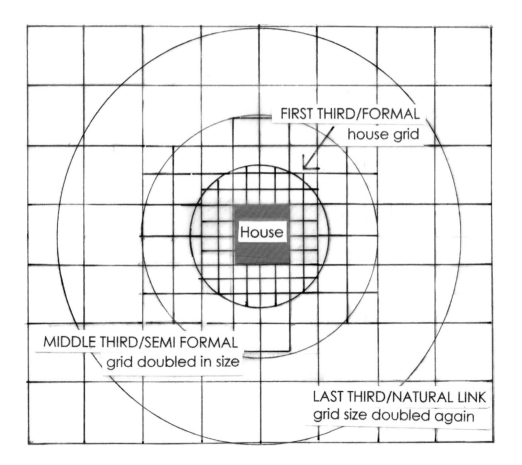

FIRST THIRD/FORMAL
house grid

House

MIDDLE THIRD/SEMI FORMAL
grid doubled in size

LAST THIRD/NATURAL LINK
grid size doubled again

This garden in Oxfordshire demonstrates how the rule of thirds can be observed. The terraces that immediately surround the formal house are also formal. Further away from the house the terraces and the plantings become more relaxed but still have an element of formality, and the furthest area of the garden includes a lake that connects the garden with the landscape beyond with its sweeping curves, rough mown grass areas and informal plantings.

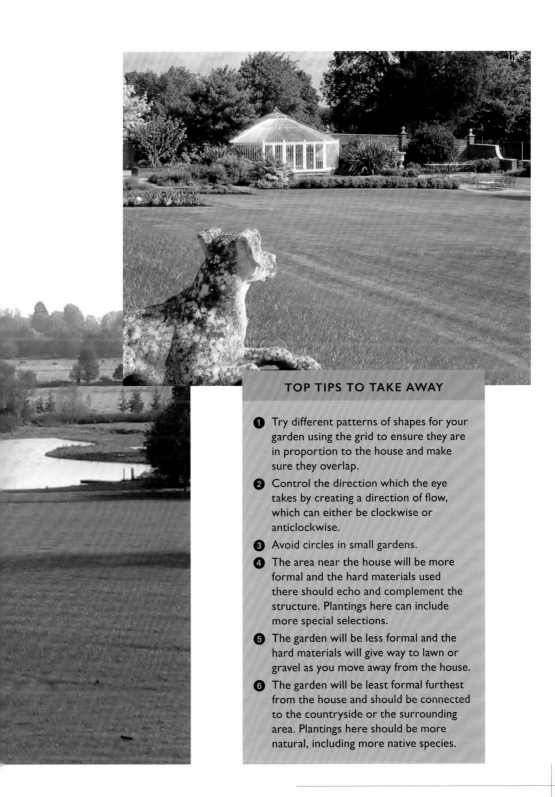

## TOP TIPS TO TAKE AWAY

1. Try different patterns of shapes for your garden using the grid to ensure they are in proportion to the house and make sure they overlap.

2. Control the direction which the eye takes by creating a direction of flow, which can either be clockwise or anticlockwise.

3. Avoid circles in small gardens.

4. The area near the house will be more formal and the hard materials used there should echo and complement the structure. Plantings here can include more special selections.

5. The garden will be less formal and the hard materials will give way to lawn or gravel as you move away from the house.

6. The garden will be least formal furthest from the house and should be connected to the countryside or the surrounding area. Plantings here should be more natural, including more native species.

Having described the method by which one can attain a well-proportioned design, John leads his audience back to the 'rule of thirds'. In this last lesson, he revisits the appropriate use of materials in different contexts.

## MORE ON THE RULE OF THIRDS

My last lesson ended in explaining the rule of thirds to you, and in my final lesson of 'An Introduction and First Steps in Garden Design', I would like to return to where we left off and take you through a recap of what we have covered before showing you how I put the theory into practice.

At the risk of being tedious, I will repeat the rule of thirds because it explains not only the shapes to use in planning your design as it moves away from the house, but also the materials you might use to build it and lastly, of course, the plantings which you put into it.

The theory starts with the basic grid taken off the proportions of the house. Against the house this can be broken down again by halving, even quartering, the grid proportion to encompass small detail and paving.

But as you move away from the house the grid can double, and even go further if the farthest parts of your garden are seen against a distant view, or more modestly against a tall wooded backdrop or even a big overhanging tree – because you are beginning to think three-dimensionally by now and by thinking about future sizes in the fourth dimension of time as well.

A town house with proportions clearly linked to the house.

### APPLYING THE RULE OF THIRDS
In the first example, the goal was to make over the garden of a period house for a young couple with two boys.

Quite a lot of space was needed for entertaining and much of the lawn area was paved with brick or stone. (The stone was there already.) Three steps lead up to a small grassed area for the boys to kick a football. While there is plenty of room for a table to eat out on the terrace, wooden bench seating has also been built in to border the three steps up between old apple trees. There is a small ramp as well for the mower.

Much of the planting in this south-facing

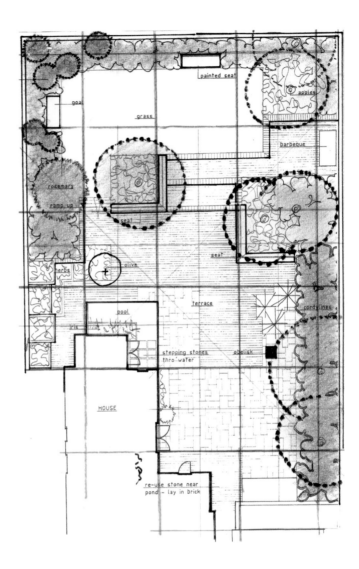

The following labels appear within the plan:

painted seat

apples

goal

grass

barbeque

rosemary

ramp up

herbs

seat

olive

seat

terrace

cordylines

pool

iris

stepping stones
thro' water

obelisk

HOUSE

re-use stone near
pond - lay in brick

The design steps up to
a grassy play area for the
clients' two young boys.

garden existed, but a group of tall conifers on the top left-hand side is suggested
to block the view from a neighbouring house.

You can now use fairly standard ways to reproduce different paving
techniques and broad planting masses on your plans. You can shade areas to
create a feeling of enclosure in the garden as well: the darker the shading or
colour, the bulkier the plants. I mark the position of standard trees and indicate
the width of their heads.

I am also moving away from just pattern to accurate draughting for the width
of steps, the size of a seat and so on. I am working to scale, in fact; the scales I
mainly use are 1:50 or 1:100, depending on the size of the garden.

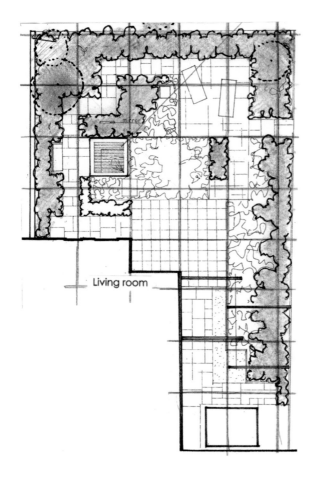

Living room

LEFT A Continental garden in which the grid proportions clearly derive from the proportions of the house.

RIGHT Notice how the squares of the grid grow larger the further away they are from the house in this semi-formal garden plan for a house in the country. This reflects the proportional transition from the smaller scale near the house to the larger scale as the garden flows towards the countryside.

BELOW RIGHT Sympathetic plantings in the form of natives or plants with habits that blend in with the surroundings can help make a garden feel at home in its setting. Here you can see the difference between mown and unmown grass.

The small garden in the next example (above) is in Germany – it is located in town and is a modern terrace house, so has neighbours on both sides. The garden looks out on to a small public park to which the owners have a gate. They are enthusiastic gardeners with no signs or mention of children. The garden gets the sun all day, and while a terrace area was necessary outside the living room for convenience, an evening sun terrace was also located across the heavily planted flower garden. A small pool and fountain provide a feature from the inside of the house.

On the right-hand side of the garden a pergola runs from the house to the boundary fence and gives privacy for the kitchen door and service area from the neighbour's house.

One grid covers this whole area, but the pattern doesn't always stick to the grid. The proportions it outlined, however, have been adhered to. Remember the grid is used to get your eye into a system of proportions that work back to the proportions of the house it adjoins.

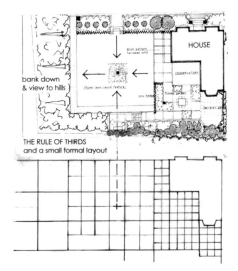

bank down
& view to hills

HOUSE

CONSERVATORY

THE RULE OF THIRDS
and a small formal layout

In the third example we look at the layout of a semi-formal garden at the side of a period house.

The terrace area runs round a conservatory extension, which sits in the angle of this L-shaped house, and which is the basis of its grid. You can see how the large grid size breaks down to form a detailed terrace. From the terrace runs a simple square lawn, with an axis running to a central sculptural feature.

Beyond the lawn, the ground falls sharply away to a view of distant hills, at which point the grid size goes back to the original. So there is a clear proportional transition from small-scale domestic detail to a larger scale landscape view. The transformation from domestic to countryside beyond is not only a difference of scale but can also be achieved with sympathetic planting.

The fourth example is a garden belonging to one of a pair of former farm cottages looking directly on to fields through a boundary hedge. A sheltered area is tucked in at the side of the house, and is covered with a pergola. This is the first third of the layout.

This sort of design is often suggested by existing trees and shrubs already on site. The second third of the plan – the central area – is defined by two existing silver birches which provide lovely light summer shade, but also make a feature in winter with their silvery stems. They are surrounded by a rougher grass area, which has spring bulbs in it as well. And this treatment is repeated against the far field boundary – the third part where gardening has become much wilder, being part of the landscape surround.

My final plan is of quite a complex layout which uses up part of an awkward triangular garden to provide extra off-street parking at the other side of the newly constructed

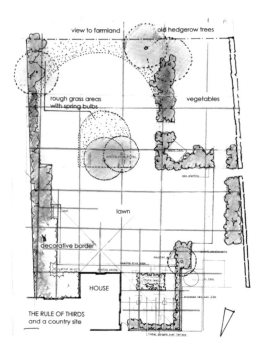

The design of this country garden (above) was suggested by the trees and shrubs on site but relies on the rule of thirds as it transitions from house towards the countryside.

The angle of the grid pattern was adusted outside of the wall to accommodate the triangular shape of the garden.

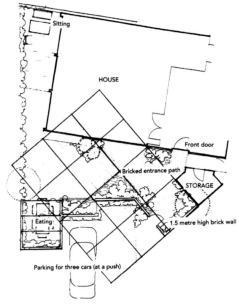

This front garden in upstate New York takes into account the challenges of the site including deer and snow (it includes underground heating) and is consistent with the rule of thirds as it transitions to the parking area beyond.

wall. The same grid proportion, taken from the house extension, was used to define both the parking area and the courtyard, but with an adjustment to the angle.

### FRONT GARDENS

I am all too conscious of not having brought front gardens into my lessons, but they are often dominated by the cars that use them, and increasingly in urban situations owners are removing anything decorative to allow for off-street parking. Too many people use hard paving for this purpose, which causes flooding of roadside drainage with excess water runoff. Surface your parking spaces with a permeable hard surface to avoid this.

My first example of a front garden in upstate New York has a small pedestrian 'precinct' at a high level off its parking area which leads to the front door. As it faces north and is visited by deer, the whole area is paved, other than marginal planting with a central feature of a multi-stemmed birch and a group of boulders. But the steps are wide and generous with their proportions in conjunction with those of the elevation of the house.

The real beauty of the rule of thirds is that it is relevant to any size of garden and broadly in any country in the world. In larger town gardens the second of the thirds will come into play as well. But only in the largest country gardens can you use all the thirds where the garden goes beyond the influence of the house and the surrounding countryside takes over. In small urban spaces surrounded by fences of other buildings, only the first of these thirds will be relevant.

## SELECTING MATERIALS

As the pattern for the garden which you evolve changes according to the rule of thirds, so does the hard material which you use.

Materials round the house tend to be remarkably similar throughout the developed world; it is only as you move into the outer edges of a garden that a local vernacular idiom sometimes becomes applicable. The local vernacular can work as well in conjunction with older properties.

Always consider what is your local paving material, gravel or chipping. It will certainly be cheaper than an imported material. In many areas, of course, there is not a local stone but you have clay from which bricks and tiles are made. If you use these, always check that they are hard enough to take the wear you propose and, in cold areas, that they are frost proof. When laid in a fairly random sort of way, stone walling reflects the countryside so is more appropriate outside the city.

This is not the place to go into the details of laying hard materials, but ensure they are laid on a sound base and that they drain well.

This is more a catalogue of materials which you might use.

ABOVE LEFT AND RIGHT Stones for both walling and paving are very much part of the local idiom where they are available.

LEFT Stone paving can reflect the basic grid and be infilled with paving brick. Paving bricks or pavers are thinner and sometimes slightly larger than building bricks and are certainly much harder.

Timber decking is a popular surface material but should be well laid and of an appropriately hard wood for your area. It can be used to surround swimming pools and looks good in what would be the middle third of a larger layout.

Garden paths can be laid in any number of types of pebble or gravel. The former can be from the beach or river-washed so is usually rounded. Gravel is a chipping from a larger stone which has been crushed. It is important to lay gravel and roll it into a stable base. It shouldn't be crunchy and difficult to walk upon.

Another medium particularly good for paths in a wooded area is pulverized bark, which gives a soft, springy feel underfoot.

Both bark and gravel will often be edged in timber, brick or concrete kerbing.

In these four lessons on steps to designing your garden. I have given you a huge amount of information, and the basic step-by-step rules are applicable generally, I believe, in most situations round the world.

I have tried to explain the underlying principles on which I base a garden design, though each design will probably be different for nearly every site round the world. How we use the space will vary accordingly to climate and site conditions. But it is we, the users, who remain remarkably constant and who are the common denominator in resolving the layout of the garden.

As you get into garden design you will find that you learn as you go along, but the overriding rule is to keep it simple and well proportioned. Enjoy!

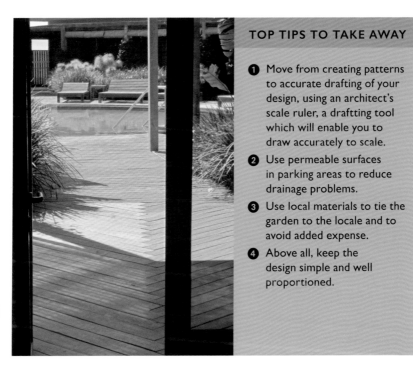

Timber decking is a useful alternative in the middle third of a larger layout if it is well constructed from durable wood.

## TOP TIPS TO TAKE AWAY

1. Move from creating patterns to accurate drafting of your design, using an architect's scale ruler, a draftting tool which will enable you to draw accurately to scale.

2. Use permeable surfaces in parking areas to reduce drainage problems.

3. Use local materials to tie the garden to the locale and to avoid added expense.

4. Above all, keep the design simple and well proportioned.

John will always be remembered for protesting that he was not a 'planty' person and that plants came last in his designs. Nevertheless, anyone who accompanied him to a nursery or garden centre, especially near his home, knew that he loved certain plants tremendously. Anyone who worked with him or studied under him learned to think of plants first as mass then detail (think herbs). He argued that plants were the last component he incorporated into his design for the same reason that an interior designer would add the details like cushions, curtains and chairs after having developed the big picture.

In addition to stressing the importance of choosing plants that are suitable for the conditions and climate of a specific garden, John developed a five-category system of planting that was easy for his students and clients to comprehend. He began with his 'specials', which were the large trees, or in some cases shrubs, that were already on site. The question was what stayed and what was removed based on the design. If the garden was new, the specials have to be selected, again in accordance with the design.

Developing the skeleton, or bones, of the garden is next, usually comprised of shrubs, some trees, usually evergreen, that help create structure year round. The infill are the shrubs and perennials that serve a decorative function.

The 'pretties' come next, destined for the front of the border, or are core plants combined with grasses. Finally comes the 'flotsam', a broad category encompassing bulbs, ferns, ground-covering plants, climbers and even annuals in pots.

This lecture to a Japanese audience explains the process of creating a sustainable and manageable planting design.

Above all, John emphasized the importance of having a plan prior to buying plants as the best way to ensure you don't come home with plants that don't suit your site or your design.

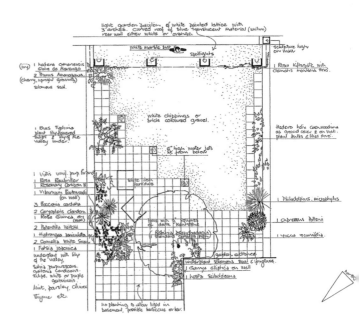

# FIRST STEPS IN PLANTING DESIGN

This morning I want to talk about putting plants together to create a particular look. The look will have something to do with the location of the garden – whether in city, suburb or country – and it will also have something to do with both the period of the house, its age and of what it is built.

You can, of course, fight the location – creating a cottage garden in town, for instance – but you are making the job more difficult for yourself, as whatever the look you want to achieve, it has to be possible in growing terms and then subsequently in maintenance terms as well. Flights of fancy are all very well, but they are expensive both financially as well as in time.

A term which the great French architect Le Corbusier used applies to this and all other areas of garden design generally. It was 'less is more'. Carry that with you and remember it!

Before seeking to fill your garden with exotic plants at random, remember that where you are now was once natural vegetation which extended from the smallest moss, through herbs and perennials to shrubs and then trees – which in ecological terms is known as the 'climax vegetation'.

LEFT Before going to the garden centre or nursery to buy plants for your garden, be sure you have a good plan and that you stick to it.

RIGHT Whether or not you use natives, make sure you plant what will grow well in your area and make your plantings proportionally bold.

Creating a garden involves pushing aside this natural vegetation to create a different set of layers or horizons, which we seek sustain altogether. Gardening is the practice of restricting plants from doing their natural thing, which for a climax of trees is to develop and blot out what grows beneath. Naturally, trees die, fall and in the resulting open glade a new cycle begins as growth recommences. I'm not suggesting we follow this cycle, but it is worth remembering. It's also important to know your light conditions. If you work with nature by selecting the plants that want to grow in your soil and aspect, you are likely to succeed.

None of this has much to do with putting plants together, but it does provide some background thinking not only to your plants and your gardening, but to your life too – it's a holistic approach.

Finally, the merit of a plant need not only be its flower and its colour, although modern horticultural writing does emphasize this. As a garden designer I am interested in the look of a plant for 365 days a year, not just for the duration of its flowering.

The smaller your garden, the more each plant plays a part. If the Japanese garden has taught the West anything, it is its seeming tranquillity and lack of flower colour; green is a perfectly acceptable colour!

See what grows locally in other gardens and pick garden forms of what grows wild near you if you live in the country. Start to learn about plants in a nursery garden or botanic garden, but take a directory or commercial catalogue with you to check and mark what you see, so you know that it is commercially available. Then when thinking of flowers, remember to consider their fragrance.

Start to categorize your plants as you might use them – and list what you like under those categories: trees, bones (the shelter and screening plants, usually

Select plants that provide interest in more than one season. Flowers are not always the priority!

Coloured stems are a fantastic way to brighten up long winter months.

The size and shape of a plant, leaf colour and texture make a garden interesting in all seasons.

evergreen), infill, decoratives (includes everything from ground-cover roses to rosemary and euphorbias), and 'pretties' (like bulbs – masses of them).

Last, in your groupings remember the word 'scale'. The scale of a mass of any one plant should read against the scale of background shrubs, the height of the rear wall or fence, the width of the lawn, the height of a neighbour's trees or the length of a view. The bigger the scale of these surrounding elements, the larger the scale of your masses, and the larger the elements of the whole design. Keep the effect simple and positive. Too many little bits of this and that – as pretty as they may be – do not add up to a total effect.

If you are having trouble, the chances are that you have the wrong plant, so try again. Gardens never finish – that's the pleasure of creating them.

In addition to not being 'planty' John averred he was not 'watery', though he did use water in his designs not infrequently. One of the first two projects he undertook at Denmans after he took up residence was the creation of a circular pool (1982) and a second, more organically shaped pond (1984) which he built in collaboration with the water gardener Anthony Archer-Wills. When John did use water in his designs it served multiple functions. Besides reflecting light and the sky and attracting wildlife, he often used the shape and position of a pool to connect architecture to garden or garden to the larger landscape: a small square reflecting pond beneath a giant beech tree, a circular pool to pull the geometry of a rural landscape into the garden he was designing, or a pond with bold curves in proportion to the landscape around it. The relationship of the water with the land and the climate and the vegetation drove his design in each case.

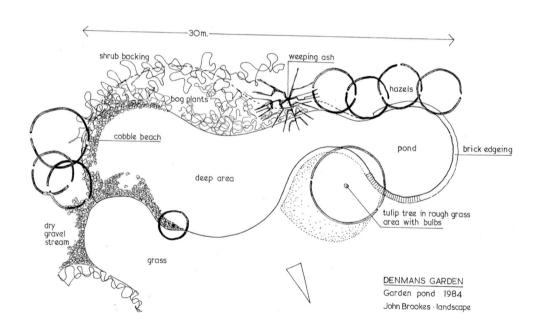

30 m.

shrub backing

weeping ash

hazels

bog plants

cobble beach

pond

brick edgeing

deep area

tulip tree in rough grass area with bulbs

dry gravel stream

grass

DENMANS GARDEN
Garden pond 1984
John Brookes · landscape

ABOVE A plan of the pond John built with Anthony Archer-Wills at Denmans is an example of how John relied on geometry to link shapes in the garden.

RIGHT A waterfall in this Polish garden adds sound and shimmering light and, seen through large glass doors, relates the swimming pool concealed beneath this terrace to the garden beyond.

## HOW I USE WATER AS A DESIGNER

I am not a very watery sort of person. I positively loathe trickly little streams prettied up with marginals in a domestic garden setting called 'naturalistic'. Perversely, though, I like the dry stream bed 'look' with watery type plants growing in it.

So how do I rationalize this dichotomy? Someone more informed on the subject would probably say I was alienated from water in childhood – and when I remember being invited to come on into the North Sea in summer, I think that they would be right!

But I have always enjoyed wider landscapes and the place of water in them – the glassy plane of a lake or the chattering of a rushing mountain stream. Near my home now there are brimming clear chalk streams with strands of water weed swaying in the current. Water on a large scale, therefore, I do enjoy – so proportion and scale help determine my feelings.

I think that I am saying that I find the transposition of a natural watery look (whether rushing or still) into a reduced garden setting difficult, and usually unconvincing, not only in its scale but often its siting too. Few garden ponds seem correct, as they are obviously not positioned as nature would, and as one of our basic elements water needs very careful handling in its surround.

Some years ago, I wrote a book on Islamic gardens, having spent time in southern Spain, northern India and Iran where I worked. In these hotter parts of the world, and in the context of the Moorish and Mughal garden, I really saw how formalized water was used, both functionally and symbolically and on both the palatial and private scale. In my own designs it is in the built environment where I am much happier with its use, no doubt because of this experience. But their water was always lit by sun and their fountain sprays sparkled and cooled the air. Of course, the same can

ABOVE Two years in Iran with a stint in India to research Mughal gardens for his book *Gardens of Paradise* increased John's awareness of the importance of water in the garden.

happen elsewhere but often doesn't in other climates. Water used with the built environment is not, I believe, quite so dominant a feature, and I therefore find it more satisfactory. However, at the end of the day, as a designer one provides only what the client wants, and what their site dictates. Personal preferences are not necessarily important.

People's attachment to the allure of water is often almost mystical, for when it is tranquil – preferably with sunlight playing upon it – water has the power to calm; it is both restorative and contemplative. But again, I think that it is difficult to achieve on a small scale, although when trying to use it, in whatever its designed form, it is this criterion which I seek to achieve. The wrong fountain, the wrong rocks, the wrong planting so easily destroy such a composition, which doesn't necessarily need decoration anyway.

Time and again I realize that while I struggle on with water detailing, nature gets it right every time in her simplicity. From her the designer – and often their clients too – can learn a lot. It's worth a close study.

RIGHT John designed a large pond and stream system in New York that Anthony Archer-Wills built, complete with two waterfalls. The result was a substantial increase in wildlife.

The idea of incorporating sculpture in a garden is ages old, and the reasons for doing so as personal as the choice of sculpture. For John, sculpture offered another opportunity to add theatricality in a garden. Here, as he draws a distinction between what is architectural rather than sculptural, he offers a few guidelines for using sculpture effectively – whether as an exclamation mark or a lowly semi-colon. Above all, the sculpture should 'fit' as a complement to the garden.

The type of sculpture you use in your garden should suit your style and site. Don't be afraid to be whimsical or to use pieces that are unconventional.

## USING SCULPTURE IN THE GARDEN

I have been thinking how I might categorize larger elements that you might introduce into a garden and it's quite difficult, as it has been my experience that anything sculptural, large or small, is subject to huge personal preference. Though there are a few rules, I think.

And to say sculptural is misleading, too, since anything large can become almost architectural (I stress almost, since we don't want to get into the realms of planning permission). Anything large can be categorized as an architectural feature which should work with something else. That something else might be a building, it might be a tree or trees, or it might be a view. Anything large in too small a space will dominate that space, and while this might work in a built enclosure, it probably won't in a small garden.

So, the feature can become a primary focal point, such as classical statuary, or secondary within an overall view, acting as a centrepiece to existing features.

As a focal point the feature can be modern or traditional statuary, either clothed with plant material or free standing. Equally, a small pavilion can be the feature, or a pier with finial ball on top, even a column.

Treated in the primary way, the features act like an exclamation mark in a sentence – but treated the secondary way it's only a semi-colon, or even a full stop before the next sentence. It all depends upon the subject of the piece.

And here's the crunch.

Few of us can rush off to a smart auction house sale and buy an enormous piece to fill a 'special' place. What we can do, however, is visit junkyards or architectural salvage yards and select what we see and place it accordingly.

I use a lot of architectural masonry which I get from a catalogue and which is made of reconstituted stone in a mould rather than carved, but once it's mossed up no one knows. Likewise, I have no compunction about using large fibreglass pieces, possibly looking like lead. If they were lead, I would need to insure them and fix them to prevent their being stolen as well.

I personally feel that if you are contemplating using a feature, in most spaces one good fair-sized piece is better than dozens of little ones. We tend to mess up a garden with bits of pots, pergolas and plants that are blobby. A garden should be restful, and your feature should complement the whole rather than scream 'look at me!'

A standard setting is the old tiered fountain in the centre of an in-and-out driveway. I personally find this a little clichéd, not to mention pretentious if the house behind it all doesn't come up to scratch. Now I'm getting bitchy, but it's all too easy with large pieces in small spaces to become a little 'over the top'.

In the right place the drama of the situation can be played up and be great fun.

'Learning to look' does not stop at the garden gate. It also applies to looking and learning from other gardens, small and large. Here John describes a small garden, from its layout to its materials to its planting, emphasizing how it associates with the interior as a room outside.

## THERE'S MUCH TO BE LEARNED FROM OTHER PEOPLE'S GARDENS

For those who have a small garden, it is very difficult to find a similar space from which to learn. For while there is always your neighbour's plot, there is then not much else before those gardens which are open to the public – and they are often too big.

It takes quite an accomplished eye to transpose and reduce a large idea down to a small space.

By learning from a garden, I mean seeing what grows where, studying the layout, seeing what materials its surfaces are made of, and so on. Other people's small gardens, when you can get into them, are as fascinating as other people's sitting rooms – and there are never two which are alike.

I would like to show you a small garden, probably not a million miles away from where you are sitting. I call it a garden, though actually it's an outside room, furnished very like the conservatory and sitting room which make up two sides of it. The third side is the neighbour's – it is a shared fence – and the fourth the wall to a local girls' school.

The size is 9 × 5 m/30 × 16 ft, and while it is south facing, the gardened bit is in the shade of the party fence. The west side of the area is dominated by an old plum tree.

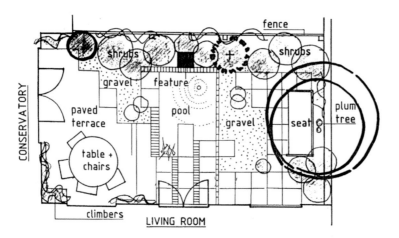

This garden plan includes texture, strong lines, detail and focal points to be enjoyed from the living room as well as the conservatory.

HOW TO DESIGN A GARDEN

It seems important in a garden of this size to hold the eye within the layout, and this has been achieved by placing a pool and fountain which centres on the French windows to the living room. Behind the pool is a piece of statuary in reconstituted stone. So, pool, fountain and statuary provide a fairly dominant feature.

The conservatory needed another eye-fixer, and a bench seat under the old plum has been painted and is seen across the pool.

The paving to the area was inherited – there is some brick work, some slabs, and a bit of paved infill with, in between, areas of consolidated or hard gravel which has random planting in it. By all the rules, this should look messy, but it doesn't since the amount of planting dominates everything else and envelops it in greenery and colour.

The main bulk of the planting on the shady side is of evergreen material screening the fence and providing winter interest – for you can't escape this area at any time from inside. There's an old bay – it grows fast as an evergreen shrub – a camellia, three ribby leafed *Viburnum davidii*, with honeysuckle and the evergreen *Iris foetidissima*.

Colour is provided by foxgloves in early summer – the white ones you grow from seed – and the autumn-flowering Japanese anemones. There is Irish yew, which will be too big in ten years' time but can be removed, and a shrubby gold catalpa having huge heart-shaped leaves and bright fresh green colour. Alchemilla and sun roses grow in the gravel, and from time-to-time lilies in pots, grown in the conservatory, are sunk in it too, bringing an amazing fragrance into the area.

I am not suggested that this is labour-free garden space, but it is wonderful for pottering in, removing the odd weed and restraining the odd branch, and in the evening, with a drink in hand, it is a little paradise, providing a focal point for the whole ground floor.

Camellias and *Iris foetidissima* are two evergreen plants that offer more than one season of interest.

# PART IV:
# THE
# CRAFT OF
# GARDENING

HOW TO DESIGN A GARDEN

# ON PLANTING

I am constantly amazed at nature's planting plan which I see as I walk my dogs daily in the woods, on the Downs or by the sea. I am always trying to interpret this casual refinement in my gardens, mixing native plants where appropriate with introduced species.

I now find the sophistication of 'the long border' at this or that property suffocating somehow – and the view of the open countryside at the end of it much more 'liveable with'.

A view from the Sussex South Downs near Denmans where John found peace and inspiration on his walks with his friends and his pugs.

Believing in the need to find 'a natural way forward', John thought that gardeners ought to take on the responsibility of planting appropriately for the climatic and ecological conditions of a site. For him, this also meant that gardeners can help support 'regional diversity' in their own locale by learning what grows naturally around them. One of the important keys to ensuring planting success is knowing the soil and what John refers to in this piece from 1995 as 'the lie of the land'. From the composition of soil to drainage, John advocates focusing on husbandry of the land and working with it, which is more relevant the larger the site. Doing so will benefit the environment, help preserve regional uniqueness and simplify maintenance.

# PAUSE BEFORE YOU PLANT

## A GARDEN IS MORE THAN A COLLECTION OF PLANTS

One of the hardest things for a gardener to do is to pause in the cultivation of plants long enough to take stock of your site. Even a new garden owner cannot wait to rush out, buy plants and get them in the ground. There is a misconception that a garden is a collection of growing things alone, and that the sooner that we start establishing them to achieve some non-focused end result, the quicker we will achieve 'a garden'. However, it's worth stopping for a moment to resolve what it is you want from your land tomorrow, next year and five years on. Longer, even, if you have a large piece of ground, for you may need to plant forest trees which become huge, and all too soon.

For a garden, of course, is a growing process – and not only does it grow but you do, too, in family size perhaps, hopefully in experience, certainly in age and, with that, maintenance capacity. One's tastes alter as well. So, there is nothing static about a garden: it's living, growing, changing and hopefully improving as it gets older. A bit like a family really, for it needs food and succour, too! But also like a family, it needs management and rules for its development, and it is these rules in a garden which are what make it work.

Now garden rules are to do with people, how they use a space, and whether they feel comfortable in it. It's all to do with proportion and convenience. The smaller the space, the more difficult it is to make it work. Probably the first mistake is to even call a small space a garden – as though one could just scale down a country garden concept using plants in miniature. Actually, a small urban space could be thought of as interior designed space but outside.

Specific plants don't come into this early computation of what a garden is about at all really, unless you are trying to design round a huge existing tree which can't be ignored; they only happen when you start to think about styling. You could style a working garden space a number of obvious ways – Japanese, Provençal or perhaps cottagey. Each conjures up a certain look in the mind's eye in the material of which it is built, its colour theme and its selection of plant material.

So, in developing a garden, there are layer upon layer of considerations which, if taken in sequence, will help you to achieve your ambition. Where things go wrong is to break the sequence or to muddle it about, and the consequent garden result shows the confusion all too obviously. Even before getting down to the basis of a garden, which is its soil, I think it is important to have thought through what a garden is all about for today. Increasingly, there is an awareness that the garden should sit easily within its site and not be at odds to it.

A garden is more than a collection of plants and it should provide peace, beauty, and a place to have a quiet moment at the end of a long day. To achieve the right garden for you, take time to plan with the long term in mind.

Since the days of grand estates and country homes, we have undergone not only a social revolution but a continuing environmental one as well, and the merits of a garden with too many alien plants are being questioned, for they are undoubtedly more difficult to maintain than natives (and where they are not, they can become invasive). That style of garden and the wide range of plants it contains are patently at odds not just with the landscape in which it sits, but with native flora as well as fauna.

As we seek a more 'natural' way in our diets and our lifestyles, why not in our gardens?

With much of this reasoning I would agree. There is a philosophy with which I disagree, however: one of suppressing the natural completely in both layout and plant material and superimposing a perceived superior and unnatural form to replace it.

Ice and snow working upon a landscape formed by eruptions of the earth created our landscapes. Knowing what kind of soil you have will help you know what kind of plants will grow best for you.

## IT'S ALL ABOUT THE SOIL

Whatever the type of garden we ultimately achieve, we are always dependent (like the old cottager) upon the soil. Now any soil throughout the world is the end product of a particular climate of rain, wind and sun working upon a basic rock over many millennia. Eventually, a soil layer develops – sometimes poor or more or less just mineral; with added humus from the degeneration of plant material upon it, workable soil is formed which creates areas of green.

Only slowly did we clear our forests to provide open land for arable crops and enclosure for grazing. It is this same type of cleared and then managed landscape in which most of us still live, or those, at least, who are fortunate enough to live in the countryside. Yet beneath the city streets as well, just a tiny space below the pavement, is soil, and we are wafer thin upon its surface.

When we talk of creating a home, we say that we are 'putting down roots' – that is, we are settling or growing into our particular spot. And it's sobering to realize that no matter where you live, it was probably forest once, and that you are tapping into the same soil which produced it.

Thought of in this fundamentally earthy way, and in a world where the countryside and woodlands are fast disappearing under the developer's advance, the need to preserve in some measure our regional diversity is essential. And you in your own garden can help to do it, and the sum total of others doing the same thing can be enormous. After all, you live in an area because you like the look of it. Why turn everywhere into a garden centre manager's dream of rockery, plastic pool, dwarf conifer and heather?

This is overstating my case, I know, but fantasies have a nasty habit of becoming realities, and on the one piece of ground which you own you have the opportunity to do something about it, so that your gardening isn't superficial. It is really land husbandry; good and basic stuff which extends the feeling of what you have very expensively bought (and are probably still paying for) rather than imposing something alien upon it.

Maintenance as we've seen is now a buzz word. Go with the lie of your land and you'll make life easy. Fight it and it's double the work. And I believe this to be true of every garden plot – I am not directing this to the exclusive owners of vast acres.

The soil which you work is, of course, the key to the garden you can devise in terms of not only what you can grow but also its character, and how you can deal with changes of level or a damp place.

Start from the point that no matter how bad you think your soil is, it will naturally grow something, unless it has been chemically polluted (and happily domestically there isn't too much of that about – yet). We used to call what grows first, after soil disturbance, annual weed (which is actually encouraged by cultivation). If you left that alone (and I'm not suggesting you do), from it another generation of native perennials would emerge. The description 'weed', notice, has now become 'native'. Then from the perennials you would get shrubs and eventually small trees going all the way up to forest vegetation – the natural state before we farmed the land so intensively. So, each soil and situation originally had its own range of plant material. Ecologically, this build up from perennial to forest tree is called a plant profile. Once you understand what your particular profile might have been, the challenge is not necessarily to copy it in your garden, but to use it as a yardstick.

By taking the time to do some research and to understand the attributes of your site, you will not only save yourself time and money, you can help preserve the uniqueness of your region.

## DETERMINING YOUR PLANT PROFILE

To research into what grows naturally you must visit a local wood (if you have wooded ground) or an open space which might be waste, even a roadside verge, if your garden gets full light. Railway embankments are increasingly becoming most wonderful wildlife habitats, since nobody disturbs them for years on end. You will need a wildflower, shrub and tree book to help you identify what you see, and you will be amazed at the names (usually the Latin ones) which you start to recognize as being similar to plants in your own garden. For you are looking at the original species of which the gardened variety is a cultivar.

Taking specific soil types and readily identifiable locations, let's look at open chalky land, then shadier. Now alkaline chalk, which is considered very difficult and nonproductive in the garden, has one of the richest natural vegetations, where it has been grazed, of wild annual and perennial flowers. Even on roadsides with this soil type you will see forms of sneezewort (achillea) and chamomile (artemisia), bellflower (campanula), columbine (aquiligea), cranesbill (geranium), ox-eye daisy (leucanthemum), ragged robin (lychnis), evening primrose (oenothera), cowslip/primrose (primula) and masses more. The original species all growing in the cottage garden.

Take reference books with you when you walk through the landscape and learn the names and habits of the plants that grow there.

Where the site becomes shadier beneath native juniper, whitebeam or wild cherry, you will also find growing forms of the guelder rose (*Viburnum opulus*), wayfaring tree (*V. lantana*), field rose (*Rosa arvensis*), wild privet (ligustrum), and growing through them swathes of traveller's joy (*Clematis vitalba*). There might also be yew (*Taxus baccata*) and box (buxus) but little will grow beneath them.

Now there is quite a range of plants which the gardener knows, and given a chalky soil it is perhaps the cultivars of this range which the gardener could be exploring when selecting plants for the garden.

At the other end of the soil spectrum, if garden has a sandy (usually acid) soil, which the gardener enjoys as it is so easy to work, nature's range is far thinner for sandy soil is actually a poor and hungry medium. Where open areas are more heath than meadow, heather and ling thrive, with fine grasses, harebell (campanula), knapweed (centaurea), teasel (dipsacus), purple loosestrife (lythrum), mallow (malva) and foxglove (digitalis). The shrubby vegetation might include blueberry (vaccinium), bramble (rubus), broom (cytisus), field maple (*Acer campestre*) and dog rose (*Rosa canina*). Above the shrubby profile, mountain ash (*Sorbus aucuparia*) grows with forms of willow (salix), dogwood (cornus), silver birch (*Betula pendula*) and Scots pine (*Pinus sylvestris*).

A fairly standard complaint of the gardener is that the soil is 'just clay'. With cultivation, which is heavy going, clay can become extremely productive; in the wild plenty grows upon it and no one is digging that! Of course, a clay soil can be either acid or alkaline or somewhere in the middle so its vegetation may include plants from either of the above categories, along with another range since quite often it is waterlogged at certain times of the year as well, or it might be in woodland shade.

Starting with the woodland first, which is known as the climax vegetation, ash (fraxinus) is fairly common through the whole country, along with oak (*Quercus robur*), beech (fagus), silver birch, wild crab apple (*Malus sylvestsis*), wild cherry (*Prunus avium*), mountain ash and various forms of willow. In damper clay you might see alder (*Alnus glutinosa*) and aspen (*Populus tremula*).

Of the shrubby material, elder (*Sambucus nigra*) is common in all but the highest parts of the country, along with hawthorn (*Crataegus monogyna*); hazel (*Corylus avellana*) was produced as an early coppicing tree since it will grow anywhere. Holly and honeysuckle are fairly ubiquitous, too, along with dogwood (*Cornus sanguinea*) in the south.

Of wild flowers those liking a damper situation are bugle (*ajuga*), lady's mantle (*Alchemilla vulgaris*), cuckoo pint (*Arum maculatum*), dropwort (filipendula), globe flower (trollius) and sweet violet (*Viola odorata*). Then there is a huge range of native ferns to call upon for cool damp situations.

In actual boggy ground we have water avens (geum), marsh marigold (*Caltha palustris*), water forget-me-not (myosotis), water mint (mentha), the yellow flag (*Iris pseudoacorus*) and lots of reeds and rushes.

There is also a good range of bulbs we sometimes overlook as our natives: the Tenby daffodil and the Lent lily, winter aconite, snowdrop, fritillary, bluebell, snowflake and Solomon's seal.

Once you have identified the plants that grow well locally, you can add non-native or even exotic plants. Whatever you do, make sure you have a plan based on your research before facing the temptations of the garden centre or nursery. There is nothing more frustrating than purchasing a rhododendron or camellia only to discover that your soil is too alkaline for them to thrive. Avoid any plants that are invasive in your region.

Now nature's plant profile – on whatever the soil is – built up in succession from small herb through to forest tree. What we seek to do in the garden is to create an unnatural state whereby we push aside the native (trying to keep the naked soil we expose 'clean') and improve a whole profile from perennial through to tree all at once, and to more or less hold it when it has achieved what we perceive as the optimum height by restricting the plants' growth. No wonder our horticultural reading is dominated by methods of restricting growth – by cultivation, lopping, pruning and even by smothering under the guise of maintenance. What the gardener seeks to do is pervert the course of nature.

But being moderate in all things (very boring), I believe that there is a middle way.

By assessing your site, and particularly its soil, you have at the back of your mind the range of plants which would grow naturally upon it. By not straying too far from this you will give yourself a guide at least to your plant selection. And this gets you to appreciate your own wild flowers and your own native species of shrub and tree. You can, of course, go left and right of this, but hopefully it will control the impulse to buy too many garish exotics totally unsuited to your site.

Knowing the local geology can also give you clues as to how well your soil will drain and the type of hard materials, like shingle and paving, you can use to connect your garden with the local vernacular.

## IT STARTS WITH GEOLOGY

To go further into understanding what determines soil types, their texture and colour, you need a broad understanding of the geology of your country.

The shape or topography of our landscape has evolved over millions of years; the earliest igneous rocks were thrown up from the core of the earth by volcanic eruptions. These eruptions continued, though to a lesser degree, causing an ebb and flow to the sea. Successive periods of ice coverage then started to affect the landscape by glacial movement, rounding off hilltops and creating huge valleys of drift formation.

Our landscapes vary due to the remarkable diversity of ages and types of rock which formed the skeleton of the landform before the ebb and flow of sea and ice worked upon it. For in its journey the sheet ice picked up rock fragments with sand and gravel to deposit them elsewhere later. Left behind was harder, more resistant rock.

When the ice finally receded, these drift materials, as they were called, were dropped where the ice melted and were quite alien to the bedrock beneath them. The harder rocks which did not move became our mountain ranges and highlands, while the deposits of boulder, clay and gravel became the final shape and content of our lowland landscapes. Areas of chalk are calcareous deposits from ancient seabeds, made up of myriads of crustaceous sea creatures.

So, soil is derived from one of the parent rocks – whether drift or solid –

and by the action of weather upon it: rain, frost and sun. Soil itself is made up of particles of various grades known as sands, silts or clay with humus from organic debris, air and water.

The different types of rock, therefore, create the different colour and consistency of our soils – and whether it is suitable for building, and the types of building that were traditionally put upon it. This different regional architectural character all stemming from the base rock is known as vernacular architecture. The differing plant associations too, whether the land was forested or not, were a contributing factor to the vernacular, since timber was available for shingling for instance, and for fences and gates.

Beneath your topsoil the layers of parent rock are still in various stages of breakdown and refinement through clay, pebble, shale, chalk, stones and/ or boulders until the solid core is reached. Usually, the deeper the layer of topsoil, the more fertile it is, being richer in humus or organic matter and the mineral elements which are necessary for healthy plant life. A rich soil is alive with micro-organisms which constantly aid the biological process of natural decay. And that is why when we remove vegetation and natural leaf fall, which would decompose over time, it is necessary to supplement the deficiency with introduced organic matter such as manure or compost.

Some of the underlying sublayers will be permeable both for drainage and anchorage for a plant's roots; others will not when the ground above becomes waterlogged. Waterlogging happens far more often, however, on a domestic scale, when the layers beneath the topsoil have been brought to the surface during excavation and have then been consolidated by machines on a newly developed site – or simply walked upon. Digging a simple hole will soon reveal the true soil profile beneath the imposed surface layer.

Acidity or alkalinity is dependent upon what is beneath your soil. This is fairly simple to diagnose by what is growing, if you know your plants. Failing that, soil testers are available on the market which will register pH values in colour variations. Extremes of acidity or alkalinity in a soil restrict the range of plants which can be grown – but curiously help create the strongest vernacular idiom.

Other drainage factors, or degrees of coldness, are just as likely to inhibit growth as pH value. While it is possible to adjust a soil's pH, it's a fairly pointless exercise I feel, for eventually the roots will penetrate into the unadjusted area. The standard adjustment is to add a peat-like substance to a chalky soil for growing acid-loving azaleas and rhododendrons with heathers. It is far easier to establish the 'wrong' plants isolated in pots or tubs of ericaceous compost on a terrace and care for them that way.

As well as the acidity or alkalinity of a soil, its condition is also important. A coarse-grained soil is usually sandy (often acid too), while a clay or silty soil made up of small grains is called sticky or colloidal. The clay soil consequently drains badly, is poorly aerated, heavy and cold, while the sandy soil – being more open – warms up more quickly and drains well; it is light and often poor for the good drainage leaches out all the plants' nutrients as well.

A plant gets its nutrients in soluble or liquid form from a bubble of moisture contained round each grain of soil. Air is also part of the necessary equation. In a light soil the gardener seeks to hold nutrients, while a clay soil needs to be opened so that the plant can get its roots into it and allow air between the grains as well. Either way, organic matter will condition and improve soil, and for a new gardener, particularly on a disturbed virgin site, the incorporation of some form of organic matter at an early stage is vital. The decaying strands of vegetation in manure or compost will bind together the light sandy soil, but it will push apart the tight, small, often waterlogged grains of clay. Organic matter also provides minerals to feed the soil.

The makeup of individual soils is quite complex, because what appears on top doesn't necessarily continue on down. So, chalk might overlay clay or gravel overlay chalk. These differing permutations will call for differing treatments to condition the soil to make it easier to work, but, very broadly, well-rotted organic matter never goes wrong. For, you'll remember, this is simply replacing what would have been the natural leaf drop from earlier vegetation which would have become organic matter as it decayed.

The darker the colour of a soil, the richer in organic matter is its content, but also the warmer it is, for it will absorb more heat from the sun. A warmer soil makes for earlier development. A handful of good soil should be crumbly – friable is the correct term – dark and smell quite fresh. By the continued addition of organic matter to a soil over a long period you can bring even the poorest soil into 'good heart'.

I am very conscious when writing about soil that much of the terminology – 'friable', 'in good heart' – is that of the cultivator, bringing to mind the double-dug Victorian vegetable garden, which seems to have caught popular imagination. To the later conservationist gardener, however, their intensive and expensive method of husbandry is anathema. They did all this work to grow exotics in the main, or excessively sized domestic vegetables for the show stand. Always remember that in the wild nature doesn't dig, her organic canopy takes generations to develop, and there is no such thing as a weed. Nature abhors a void and she will try to fill it up with squatters as soon as possible. It is these quick squatters, which would quickly be engulfed by more permanent plants when left to their own devices, which we call 'weeds'. Nature would get rid of them just as quickly as we would. How much groundsel or ground elder do you see on a heath or in a wood?

RELATING THE GARDEN TO ITS SETTING

Once you have established the parameters of some sort of philosophy for your garden's development based upon your soil, think about what the cottage gardener in your area would have built with: a fence, outhouse, steps, a path, and how it might have been edged. You might well not be able to afford the same stone or the brick, but you might afford the next best thing in sympathy with your region. I can hear the owner of a new brick box in a suburb saying, 'But there are no cottages left here to see.' Try an older churchyard then, take a walk on the local heath or in the woods and just look. Be negative even and decide what definitely would not be right and try to work backwards from there.

The larger your site the more influence the region should have upon the lie of your particular land and in the realization of a garden. Smaller sites will start to relate the material of their layouts to the house itself, in brick or stone selection, in the colouring of walls, in whether the roof is slate or tile, and so on. These are the colours and textures you will consider for a terrace, steps, footpath edging or drive surfacing.

But before the design detail, pause to think a moment longer. Remember that a garden is with you for quite some time and it is as well to get the look of it correct from the start, although one of the nice things about a garden is that you can change it – though at a cost.

We've considered your broad landscape and in outline how it developed, and then the soil and what it will grow naturally. Scaling down again, think more specifically now about your particular plot and start to build up a site assessment. When designing a garden on paper, one of the determinants of your ultimate plan, along with what you want, is what the site is telling you. Cutting down and cutting out on an older site can both open it and let air into it, completely transforming the feel of the place. There was a vogue in the past for conifers – if these have now grown to 15–18 m/50–60 ft high, they may be too tall for the width of the site. The removal of these gloomy sentinels

On a scale plan of the garden, start to note down what views are beyond the site, both good and bad. The word 'view' conjures up rolling vistas, but often you can just see a neighbour's pear tree in flower or catch a glimpse of a spire.

can work wonders. The same has to be said about the ubiquitous planting of a leylandii hedge. Again, this grows to enormous heights and will only stand restraining for so long.

Often evergreen hedges were planted to keep out the wind, for with views out go winds in, particularly if you live in an exposed position or near the sea. So before felling anything, ask yourself why it was planted. Often the necessary screen has now become far too high and could be reduced in its height by half. Wind can be reduced, as long as it's not gale force, by filtering it. Some standard trees with a light head near the house can often filter wind just as well as a tall hedge planted a distance from it.

In urban situations, views into your garden can be disturbing. The solid fence or hedge is one way of blocking the view, but you might also consider using plantings as baffles within the site which allow for a degree of spatial flow as well. Baffles may be used to block headlights if you live on a corner site or help to cut down on traffic noise.

Again, by cutting down taller, older vegetation you may allow more sun into your site, for its orientation and how much you get (or even want) will affect your subsequent layout. Remember that if you live in a town surrounded by tall buildings, a sunny sheltered site in summer can become a black hole in winter when the sun never rises above your skyline. Trees on a railway bank or in a neighbouring garden can also blot the sun's low horizon.

*Knowing where the wind is least and the sun is best will help you determine where to place seating and dining areas. The style of your garden, in turn, will help you choose the style of your garden furniture.*

If you suppose the ideal garden orientation has lots of sun and little wind, is it morning, noon or evening sun? Each will affect how you use your garden. Broadly most plants prefer full sun: that is, from sunrise in the east to sunset in the west. But few sites allow this as your house or the neighbours, a big tree or the like will give partial shade at some time. Most plants can cope with this as long as they receive some hours of sunlight. Most flowering shrubs or perennials, certainly herbs, require plenty of sun – bright flower colour is an indication of this.

But equally there is another range of plants which can cope with light shade too. With shade, generally speaking, goes dryness. Again, very broadly, shade plants often have larger leaves giving them a greater area available to catch light, which is necessary for the photosynthetic process by which they convert the nutrients they have taken in soluble form from the soil into

food to grow. Colours of shade plant flowers tend to be paler, too, to show up more and attract insect life.

There is a small range of plant life which opens its flowers at night and has fragrance to attract moths. Evening primrose and nicotiana work this way and are wonderful planted near a terrace on summer evenings. But owners of many exposed new gardens in fact seek shade as a priority, to sit under but equally as a point of interest, for a pool of shade in an otherwise sunny site can be very attractive.

Wind can be a problem in smaller town gardens where draughts whizz round a corner or between two properties – or become a vortex when trapped in an enclosed space. Draughts need to be blocked – either by planting or even better by structure. The vortex effect of the walled enclosure is more difficult to deal with, as ideally shelter is needed outside the enclosure to defer the wind over the top of the garden. Perversely, if the enclosed area is small enough, as in a yard, the wind will go over the top anyway. Many urban small spaces are sheltered by neighbouring properties or their trees as well.

It's entirely possible that within a garden you have both well-drained soil as well as a boggy area which, from its dampness in winter or the amount of cracks in summer, you feel is in need of drainage. I have found that in fact few gardens need those complex herringbone systems of drainage one sees in old garden books. For starters your house is probably on the well-drained land anyway, and if enough of the surrounding area is also dry, I would not try to alter what is a natural condition. Create a watery or damp look instead. There is always the problem in low-lying land of where you drain to. Overdrainage also takes away a plant's natural food, which is, as we've seen, held in soluble form.

Far more necessary at a later stage in a layout is for a less complicated form of drainage using flexible pipe which can be run to a soak-a-way. A soak-a-way is a hole 1 m/39 inches down, being a metre cube itself, which is backfilled with rubble. The soak-a-way hole acts as a reservoir after rain so that accumulated surface water run-off can disperse slowly into its surrounding subsoil.

In a heavy soil, surface water may be picked up this way from a terrace, for instance, or at the base of a level change. Only in few gardens would this early detailed planning be necessary. It probably goes without saying that you should not dig a soak-a-way too near the house, as you could undermine its foundations. To be safe keep a soak-a-way at least 5 m/16 ft from the house. Houses which sit on a hill have more serious problems with their levels, for while water flows away from the house, the flow moves to the area below. So how one treats the bank – whether as a straight fall or a series of terraces – is important, as is how you catch water run-off at the bottom.

First of all it is necessary to have a clear and level surround to the house, for its maintenance apart from anything else. In this surround there might well be foul water and even surface water drainage from the house. (Surface water can be run-off from the roof and gutters.)

The run-off from the bank below the house, however it is treated, can be picked up by drainage to the existing surface water drawn from the house. It is illegal to plug into foul-water drainage. Or it might be necessary to lay a new pipe to take the bank run-off leading the water left or right of the house, before the bank begins, and direct it to its drain.

Now the bank above the drain, and how to treat it. It really depends on the importance of the bank: is it a front approach from the road – which will need access across it – or is it a dark bit at the back of the house? What is the height of the bank and what is its gradient? What is the soil? If it's light and sandy, it tends to run, where clay or chalk holds better.

Very broadly, where a gradient is to be banked and then grassed, a degree of 30 degrees from the horizontal is advised. I think that this

Any time you need to change the level in your garden, you must remember to take into account the effect your efforts will have on drainage. This applies no matter how small or dramatic those changes are. Sometimes it is best to consult an expert before taking action.

can go to 45 degrees where the bank is of a sticky material and where it is then to be planted. Some ramblers will root as they go and hold the incline. Evergreen shrubs like junipers have horizontal forms (*Juniperus sabina* 'Tamariscifolia' is one) as do cotoneasters – *Cotoneaster dammeri* is very low, but there are also more rampant forms. Ivy is a splendid ground cover, too, to hold a bank. More decorative plants can include the climbing hydrangea (*Hydrangea petiolaris*) or rambler roses which are pegged out until they root. Ramblers can sprawl down or up a bank, and you can grow clematis through them as well.

Alternatives to grass or planting are forms of terrace, which might be appropriate where the bank is to be crossed by a path or even a drive. At this point you begin to get into engineering, and I would have any proposed structure over 1 m/39 inches in height checked by a structural engineer. The weight of damp soil pushing against a retaining wall can be enormous, and your structure – whether of reinforced concrete alone or faced with brick or stone – must have both the correct depth of foundation and be the correct thickness to do its job. This is not a job for the amateur.

How you treat your terrace and paths and steps across the site will depend upon the amount of space you have to do it. Steps can be straight up and down, or they can work laterally. Whatever the way, they should drain well, not become slippery when frosted, and be safe, with the individual risers not too high or the runs of step too long before the user is given a rest.

Mounds may be constructed in a garden using surplus soil from the excavation of, say, a swimming pool, and this saves on removing soil from the site. Make sure, however, that you remove any existing precious topsoil before you start dumping your spoil. It can be used again over the inevitable subsoil – though it will be of a thinner depth remember – for growing grass if not shrubs. Grass can grow in a topsoil depth of approximately 15 cm/ 6 inches, while shrubs need at least 40 cm/16 inches. Standard trees need an even greater depth of topsoil – 50 cm/ 20 inches and over.

## TOP TIPS TO TAKE AWAY

1. Gardens are first and foremost about how people use their outdoor space. If your garden is small, think of it as an outdoor room that is an extension of your house.

2. You can help preserve regional diversity by working with the surrounding landscape rather than creating something that looks artificial.

3. By working with rather than against your soil, native plants and climate, you will save a lot of work and help your garden thrive.

4. You can find out what kind of plants will do well in your garden by determining the type of soil you have, taking note of what grows locally and developing the plant profile for your region.

5. You can grow plants that are not suited to your soil either in pots or in specially prepared areas, but expect to spend extra time on their care.

Having worked the land in one form or another from his childhood, John's understanding of land husbandry was second nature. He believed that understanding soil, plant requirements and climatic conditions critical to the success of a garden. Here he explains to his readers the nuts and bolts of improving their soil.

## IMPROVING YOUR LOT

A good soil is the very basis of a good garden. It should have a crumbly texture to it, be dark in colour, and actually smell good if you pick up a handful. I wince at the Americanized name for it: 'dirt'.

'Yours might be, Buster,' I think. 'Mine has a soul.'

Many town gardens, particularly those which have been neglected, have a dry dusty soil, usually reeking of cats into the bargain. In an initial panic to make it more fertile the new homeowner seeks to replace it very expensively, and needlessly, for it can be returned to 'good heart' by the inclusion of organic matter. By this I mean the incorporation of well-rotted compost (homemade or bought in bags or bulk) and, even better, well-rotted farmyard manure. Both compost and manure contain not only essential plant foods but actual organic plant fibres which host a myriad of bacteria and worms which are the conditioners of your soil to create that desirable crumbly effect.

Soil, as you know, may be light and sandy or a heavy clay – with lots of textural variations in between. Its consistency is broadly to do with the size of the individual mineral grains making up the soil. A sandy soil is light because it is composed of quite large individual grains of rock which are surrounded by a layer of water in which the plant nutrients are held in soluble form. Tiny feeder roots work their way easily between them. Air also gets between the particles. A clay soil is made up of much smaller mineral grains which, if not well drained, become a mush or mud with an excess of moisture that excludes air as well. It is called a heavy soil, as you will have discovered when you try to dig it.

You may dig in your organic matter at any time from autumn until about March. Do not, however, dig in a frosted soil, as you will turn in the coldest bit and it will stay cold, insulated by the surrounding soil. Well-rotted compost may be spread on top of the soil as long as you are not trapping frost. The nutrients will penetrate downwards and the worms take down the

A good method of improving soil is simply to place organic material on top of the garden in autumn and let the worms do the work all winter. This 'no-dig' method reduces work and also helps the soil structure develop an ecosystem that retains moisture and nurtures the beneficial elements of the soil.

It is important that
the organic matter
you add to your soil
is well rotted or it will
compete with your
plants for nitrogen.

organic content. This is the way to feed plants already established and around which you should not dig.

I keep stressing that organic matter should be well rotted, and if it is not it may well rob your soil of its nitrogen content as the relevant bacteria will be expending their energies on processing material which has not broken down. Fresh farmyard manure should be stacked for at least three months before use, when the process of decomposition should kill off any weed seed content. Perennial weeds such as creeping buttercup, stinging nettle, ground elder and couch grass should not be included in homemade compost since the heat created in the process will not kill their seeds or their invasive roots.

Since a good soil is the basic medium in which our food is grown, constant organic conditioning is vital at whatever level, horticultural as well as agricultural, and far better than using chemicals. Organically grown food, you will have discovered, is a little more expensive to buy, but it is considerably healthier for your well-being.

If you asked him if he liked lilacs or paeonies, John would scoff. It wasn't that he didn't like them, but for him their bloom times were too short and the rest of the year they did nothing for him. For the most part, he found conifers too dark and generally dull. The plants he favoured generally were architectural, had long bloom times, fragrance or winter beauty. The last was especially important to him, he said, as he grew older. At Denmans there is a panoply of plants with winter interest, some planted by the garden's founder, Joyce Robinson (known as Mrs J. H.), and some he planted. At Denmans he could experiment with what he liked best and indulge his own preferences.

## WINTER INTEREST AT DENMANS

By the early 2000s I became more interested in the plants that grow naturally on the Downs, so I tend to put in native plants along the perimeters or I might put in a cultivated form of a native. I'm interested in how wild plants grow in a muddle, not tight little bundles of threes, fives and sevens – it's that self-seeding, scattery look that I like: 'glorious disarray', Joyce used to call it. A dominant feature that contributes in summer is the tall grey biennial *Verbascum bombyciferum*, which I still permit to pop up all over. And I love *Euphorbia wulfenii* (properly, *E. characias* subsp. *wulfenii*) in winter and spring.

The garden, even when Mrs J. H. was alive, had a winter beauty, for it had bones and a structure of evergreens and winter colour that make it beautiful at all times of year. Few people come to visit our garden at Denmans during winter; and yet, even in the middle of January, I could describe the garden as being 'cosy', with encompassing evergreen, variegated and even grey foliage interspersed with colourful berries and stems and, yes, flower colour too. Not a blast of colour, mind you, but occasional – so much more interesting for having rarity value. And when the winter sun warms some of the flowering plants, there is a wonderful scent as well.

Increasingly, I feel that winter interest is exceedingly important. In my work as a garden designer, I like to give my clients 'bones' to their design by planting a lot of evergreens – I prefer to avoid conifers (this is difficult in very cold climates like Chicago, upstate New York and Russia, where broad-leafed evergreen plants fail), though I love yew. The result is often a green garden in winter against which early flowering shrubs such as wintersweet, winter jasmine, *Cornus mas* and all manner of hellebores show up.

I have done even more at Denmans. Starting in mid-January, there are the sumptuous catkins of evergreen *Garrya elliptica* and, though smaller, the catkins of *Salix matsudana* 'Tortuosa' (Peking willow, now *S. babylonica* var. *pekinensis* 'Tortuosa'), a curious willow form, with twisted and contorted twigs, as well as

Winter at Denmans
is not just a study in
structure. It is about
texture, colour and
form throughout the
garden. There is always
fragrance, too, which is
so unexpected in the
cold of January.

pinky, white-trunked *Betula ermanii* and, nearby, the spectacular arching stems of *Rubus cockburnianus* overlaid with white bloom.

It is also at this time of year that some of the dogwoods come into their own, notably the yellow stems of *Cornus stolonifera* (now *C. sericea* 'Flaviramea') with dark red *C. alba*. And with sun on them, the scarlet stems of *S. a.* 'Chermesina' (now *S. a.* var. *vitellina* 'Britzensis') really catch the eye.

Evergreen *Viburnum tinus* and *V. farreri* (syn. *V. fragrans*) are good winter bloomers, the latter bearing white, scented flowers in tight clusters looking lovely against a clear blue sky. I have included a number of scented shrubs which are especially fragrant in the winter sun: *Hamamelis* × *intermedia* 'Pallida', the white-berried *Skimmia japonica* 'Fructu Albo' (now *S. j.* 'Wakehurst White'), *Sarcococca hookeriana* var. *humilis* and *Daphne odora*. But the overwhelming scent comes from the spectacular *Chimonanthus praecox* (it used to be designated *C. fragrans*), with its lemon-coloured flowers on bare wood.

Although the soil here is more or less neutral (though chalky in parts), camellias seem to thrive. I use the early white-flowering 'Cornish Snow', the scarlet 'Adolphe Audusson', and the variegated, pink-flowered *Camellia* × *williamsii* 'Golden Spangles'.

Perennial material is thin on the ground, but I grow a lot of different hellebores, like the small *Helleborus foetidus* with yellow-green flowers, the coarser *H. argutifolius* (which used to be *H. corsicus*), *H. niger* and, finally, *H. orientalis* (now *H.* × *hybridus*), which comes in colours from white to plum purple.

While I'm extolling the plants that flower so early in my garden I would like to emphasize that flower colour is not my priority in putting together a planting design. It is always the mass that interests me, for it is the bulk of the mass of plants that takes a two-dimensional plan into a three-dimensional reality, though this process obviously takes some time.

Skimmia berries and a variety of beautiful camellias brighten up the garden beginning in late autumn and continue through until spring.

Winter interest can be achieved in any climate using textured bark, coloured stems, early bulbs and good structure in a strong layout. Place plants and features with winter interest outside of windows you look through most often.

If the bulk planting is evergreen, then it gives privacy or division and interest all year round. And if I can make one mass contrast with another, so much the better. So many gardens I visit, I can only describe as having spotty planting. Each plant may be exceptional, but do they make up a grouping? It is the sum total of these groups that create the comfy, green feel I find so satisfying in winter.

Overall, one of the major qualities I try to create in a garden, and especially at Denmans, is that of tranquillity through all the seasons. I often find visitors just sitting quietly on one of the benches and reflecting. Such oases of calm are increasingly difficult to find, certainly in towns, and so the importance of a garden – particularly for older people – cannot be overestimated.

One of the hallmarks of Denmans is how lawn, paving and gravel are used seamlessly to connect a series of spaces and views. Gravel gardening was first introduced to the garden in 1970 by Joyce Robinson, who lived at Denmans from 1946 until her death in 1996. John had been using gravel in gardens since the 1960s, especially as an alternative to lawns, and when he moved to Denmans in 1980 to start the Clock House School of Garden Design and to take over the gardens, he continued to use gravel for paths and as a planting medium. In this piece, written in 2002 for an article by Noel Kingsbury for *The English Garden* magazine, John explains how he uses gravel.

## GRAVEL GARDENING

I am often asked what depth of gravel is best for planting. At Denmans we have a gravelly soil so need very little – acting as a mulch really. But in general, excavate approximately 10 cm/4 inches, backfill 9 cm/3½ inches with unwashed or binding gravel, and roll to consolidate. Now top up with a thin layer of clean gravel and roll again. The final surface should be hard, not crunchy, to walk through. Plant suitable drought-loving plants straight into this.

It is important to be sure that the colour of the gravel you use looks right with other hard materials like brick, flint or stone.

Once you get the layout right, let your plants self-sow into the gravel for a relaxed, natural look.

To edge the gravel on a new site, use brick on edge or squared concrete cubing laid in concrete so that the finished level is flush with the level of the gravel. Alternatively, you could use a timber edging (treated with a preservative) – or just a turf between the newly sown lawn and gravel area. Do not scuff the gravel on to the grass, however, if you use a cylinder mower for the grass.

I do not put a permeable sheet below the gravel to stop weeds since they will grow anyway as dirt builds up in the top surface of the gravel. In fact, I want those plants which I have selected and planted in the gravel to self-seed, as Noel points out. I pull what I don't want after rain – they come up easily.

The plants I use in the gravel to self-seed include *Sisyrinchium striatum*, *Eschscholzia californica*, *Alchemilla mollis*, anything herby and, of course, *Verbascum bombyciferum*. Perennials overwinter well in our well-drained soil.

Plant in big masses, which is a really hard exercise to force yourself to do. The masses need to relate to the scale of the width of the bed, the width of the neighbouring path, or to the height of the fence or wall beyond. When seen across a lawn, the masses will look really strong and not just be a multicoloured fuzz.

When designing a garden pattern, work on paper to a scaled plan of the garden. Then translate your small plan on to the ground using a string or a hose. Use bold curves and sections of circles, right angles wherever possible for a formal effect. Plants will not grow into jutting little corners. If it looks right on paper it will look even better in reality. Do not go straight to the hose or string phase on the ground: the scale is too big.

## PLANTING TREES AND SHRUBS

I would like to tell you something about about planting trees and shrubs.

Ideally your soil should be in suitable condition, not too wet and sticky, and not too dry or cold. The object is to set your plant, be it tree or shrub, firmly in the ground at the correct depth indicated by the soil mark left on the plant when it was lifted from the field, a bed or a pot. You should dig the hole for the plant larger and deeper than this, breaking up the base of the hole to allow for root growth. This process, and the inclusion of a layer of drainage matter as well, are important if you are preparing a hole in solid clay – otherwise it simply acts as a soakaway from the surrounding soil.

Then put in a 15 cm/6 inch layer or so of good topsoil or topsoil and organic matter mixed, even adding a handful of bonemeal.

Now gently tap your tree or shrub out of its pot, assuming you are planting the usual garden centre stock, having first watered it to ensure that as much soil as possible remains on the roots. A good root ball has a mass of fibrous root: these are the feeder roots.

If the root ball is really tight – a state known as being pot-bound – break it open and, with a fork or trowel, loosen the matt of side roots. Now carefully stand your tree or shrub in the hole and make sure that the depth is correct. You would do exactly the same for bare-rooted stock or plants which have been dug up and not potted. Some roots come with netting or sacking round them – you would place the plant in the hole and then open out the netting or sacking and gently remove it.

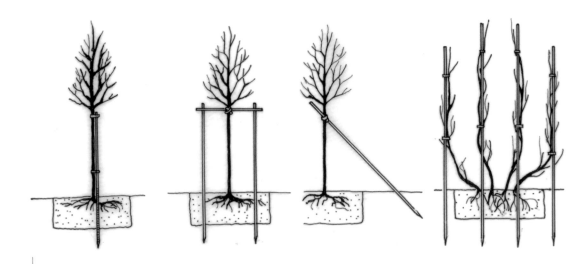

At this stage, if you are planting a tree, site your stake or stakes to hold it steady. If you plant the tree and then drive the stake in, you may remove half the roots.

Finally, stand the plant in position, start to back fill round the roots, which you have spread out as far as possible. Shake the plant up and down to facilitate the passage of soil between the roots and continue filling the hole. Occasionally, heel in the soil to firm it – not poking it, really heeling right up to the soil mark.

Hammer down the tree stake and support the tree using a plastic tree tie which you then nail to the stake. As the tree stem grows, you will need to loosen the tie in order to avoid strangling the stem.

Many newly planted shrubs benefit from being cut back after planting, so that there is not so much head to catch the wind and also to encourage root growth.

Do not be bowled along into buying plants which are too big, even when you can afford them – for, as with people, the older one is, the more of a shock to the system an operation becomes (the equivalent of a move), and the longer it takes to recover.

Aftercare of newly planted material is vital – particularly watering. It is amazing how drying spring and early summer winds can be, so check all the time. When you water give it a really good soak: at least a bucket or two per plant per week if you can't leave a hose on it for longer. Light watering only encourages surface rooting and the drying out process becomes accelerated.

You can continue planting container stock through summer, as long as you maintain it. Bare-rooted stock can be planted until the leaves appear. Conifers can be planted until about May.

LEFT Before planting new shrubs or trees, be sure your site is prepped and that you have stakes and ties on hand, along with a garden hose. Make sure you don't let the roots dry out, especially the first year, by watering deeply and thoroughly at least once a week. This will encourage roots to grow deep, which in turn will help them withstand dry spells better in future.

RIGHT This young apple tree has been staked with a simple wooden garden stake which will remain in place for 18 months. Make sure that there is space between the stake and tree or shrub so that they don't rub against one another on windy days.

## HOW TO REJUVENATE YOUR SHRUBS

I find that many people are afraid to cut back woody material since they think that they will kill the plant. The solution to doing something to the 'wretched thing' is to trim it into a rounded lollipop shape so that the growth becomes thicker and thicker and you end up with a series of balls in the garden, looking like the local parks department.

Really pruned — that is, thinned to reduce the head of the plant and its thickness at the right time of year — you in fact rejuvenate your shrub, and it takes on a new lease of life.

But what is the right time of year to give your garden this attention? Well obviously, and if you can avoid it, you do not cut back a plant just before it comes into flower. So, cut back when it has finished flowering so that you allow a full year's growing time before flowering again. It makes sense!

The winter before last I really tore into our walled garden, which was initially a mixture of both shrubs and perennials, but the shrubs had taken over, making the garden too dark for the flowering of the perennials, which generally prefer plenty of sun.

I like the look of mixed planting, because the shrub material gives interest throughout the whole year, particularly if you use decorative evergreens as well as deciduous material. By decorative evergreens I mean plants such as *Choisya ternata*, some ceanothus, forms of eleagnus, *Fatsia japonica* (in town), ilex (holly), rosemary, skimmia, viburnum forms, that sort of thing.

This fatshedera will grow back soon enough.

Just recently I tackled a tree ivy (× *Fatshedera lizei*) that makes a handsome architectural backdrop to a sculptural piece of two doves by Marie Gill. I used the birds first in a Gold Medal Chelsea Flower Show garden for the *Financial Times* in 1972, and I then took them as part payment of my fee for designing the garden.

The birds' architectural backdrop seemed to have suffered badly through last winter, so I have waded in there to cut it all back. It may look a bit naked at first but will thicken up and be fine very soon.

In another part of the garden there is a huge *Viburnum mariesii* which is ready for a cut-back, but if I do it now, when it will

flower in a month or so, I will lose its beautiful, layered white flowers. So, it will have to wait for its prune!

By mixing shrubby material with perennials, I can get a variation in size, in foliage forms, colours and textures; flower colour is a bonus on top of that.

So with pruning saw, loppers and secateurs in hand, get out there and start pruning if you have an established garden, or at least think about shaping your plants in a newer one.

The viburnum above needs to be cut back carefully to ensure it continues to look natural. The dwarf sequoia below was cut back severely but will grow back as the new growth of the species will grow on old wood. This is not true of all plants so take care to check before getting the chainsaw out.

## SUMMER PRUNING

No, don't get up. Just sit there on your terrace and look around, for now is the time to assess your garden greenery and to consider some summer pruning.

'Hell,' you think, 'I've just got over the last lot,' but now the operation is far simpler than the 'spur back to the third bud' sort of instruction. It's a general shaping up as much as anything, and a rejuvenation, since you soon forget the summer fullness of a garden once plants lose their leaves in autumn. But it's also a time to prune back spring-flowering shrubs, for if you leave it until autumn you cut off the flowering shoots for next spring.

The shrubs I am thinking about start with lilacs (syringa), which should have their flowering heads removed after they are finished when they are getting leggy; a clean amputation allows fresh young shoots to grow from the base. Mock orange (philadelphus) should have its branches thinned if they are not to become top heavy. I take the shears to broom (cytisus), giving them a short back and sides; you'll get a new head of nice tight foliage, looking good even without flowering.

Thin back the head of pyracantha. If it's becoming too rampant get right in there and cut off the unwanted branch at the main stem (you'll need gloves for this as it's very prickly). Rampant cotoneasters, kerria, even azaleas and rhododendrons I would treat in the same way.

Cutting the old wood out of your lilacs will ensure they live for many years.

Shrub roses, the catalogue tells you, need no pruning but you will find that some, after their flowering has finished, do need a shape up since long straggly branches can develop and would be better removed.

Wintersweet (*Chimonanthus praecox*) and winter jasmine (*Jasminum nudiflorum*) should have been pruned some time back, since they flower so early. I find that akebia gets out of hand as well and smothers its neighbours, so it, too, gets thinned right back about now.

As well as pruning your shrubs, you might need to look at climbers and the wall shrubs, as some may start to grow away from the wall. Prune these back flat to the wall if this is so. I would take the shears to ivy, since with maturity the plant develops a woody form when it cannot climb. You might want to reduce *Clematis montana* since it is so terribly rampant.

Wisteria may be putting out young shoots at the expense of flowering shoots next spring, so reduce these considerably, back to the second or third bud from the woody stem. *Vitis coignetiae* may be thinned as well since in maturity this can become invasive.

Do condition yourself to be bold when pruning. A gentle snip, snip is not enough. I appreciate that for the novice it takes great bravery to get in there, but you will seldom kill a plant by summer pruning it. You will need a sharp pair of secateurs and possibly some lopping shears, since your branch cuts must be clean, not dragged off.

The best time to cut wisteria back is winter but it will also need attention in summer to keep it trim.

# ON PLANTS

Inevitably, John was asked to write about plants, planting, and what he called the 'craft of horticulture'. Here are a delightful series of pieces about just that in which John expresses his views on a variety of topics.

## MY FAVOURITE PLANT

'So what is your favourite plant?' the journalists always ask.
'Favourite for where?' I rejoin. That confuses them a bit!

The furry grey *Verbascum bombyciferum*, a giant mullein, is a favourite in my own garden at Denmans, in West Sussex. It is a biennial and does well on my gravelly soil, which is more or less neutral in terms of pH. And I live near the south coast of England, so it is not a plant for everywhere, as it likes to be sunny and sheltered.

This lovely plant has other forms that are not nearly so glamorous and their yellow spikes do not grow nearly as tall. Mine get up to 2 or 3 m/7 or 10 ft, and best of all, I think, is that it self-seeds and pops up where least expected, giving that casual effect which is so hard to achieve. The seedlings can be lifted and transported very easily.

Verbascums are drought and deer resistant as well.

Giant mullein is permitted to self-sow at Denmans, providing a good punctuation point among other perennials and in a mixed border.

## A FANTASY BORDER OF VEG AND DAISIES

I have always had a fantasy dream of creating a border of flowers mixed with vegetables. I love the look of crispy winter cabbages, the gleaming stems of swiss chard and the feathery leaves of green parsley: such nice clean shapes and such neat plants! But they would need to contrast with good clear flower shapes with bright colours to create a contrasting outline, so I would stick primarily to flowers with daisy heads.

What I have in mind is a sort of cutting garden, decorative in the extreme but useful too. The advantage of having extended winter vegetable interest would be good, for many in fact are perennial, and my daisies would screen and shelter patches of vegetables that I had sown *in situ*. A disadvantage would be that I would need to work to quite a strict programme of sowing and thinning and would also need a small space for 'bringing on'. Then the border would need managing quite carefully too — not a month away at the seaside when there is cropping to be done!

First, I would need to marshall my plants, listing those vegetables and flowers I wish to include and looking up to see what flowers or does its thing when. Arm yourself with one or two good catalogues – work up to this slowly! Start to read up and make your lists over Christmas or in that dead period afterwards; it's such a cheering activity. Do not go mad in plant encyclopaedias if you are starting from scratch; you want to know that your plant selection is commercially available.

In my mind's eye I picture a good south-facing border about 6 m/20 ft long and 2.5 m/8 ft wide which I would look at directly. My soil should be light to medium loam, well dug over, and enriched with rotted organic manure or lovely crumbly compost. With the decks cleared I start to plan, approaching my plot like an artist with a clean canvas.

The prudent vegetable gardener puts his or her planting on paper first, drawing up the bed to scale.

From my list I now start to select what I would call my key plants: that is, those that have a good shape and will hold the concept together.

You can use globe artichokes throughout the garden, not just among the veg.

There are so many tomatoes available now so don't be limited to just one type.

Globe artichokes (*Cynara carduncuolus* Scolymus Group) would be excellent for this with their huge grey felted leaves. I like the French variety 'Gros Vert de Laon', of which I would buy young plants.

I have always wanted to grow blue climbing French beans too, though they turn green on boiling, and for these I would select seed of the variety called 'Purple Podded'. I would construct a small pyramidal frame for them at the rear of the border to support them and would sow these *in situ* in the spring.

A mass of crinkly grey-green seakale leaves (*Crambe maritima*) I now envision in the centre of my bed. Unforced, the shoots are as good as a spring green, or can be blanched using upturned tall terracotta pots and forced for eating in late spring. Growing seakale by seed would be slow and I would have to wait a year or two to crop it, so I would buy root cuttings or thongs of the plant and dig them in during March for forcing the following spring.

Behind my seakale I would plant a single rhubarb for its bright stems and huge leaves. This could be forced along with seakale, or I might plant a later cutting variety called 'Sutton'. Again, seed would take too long to crop, and I would buy a single crown, planting it in autumn for the following year.

For foliage contrast I would buy three asparagus roots for spring planting. For good eating I would need many more roots and would need to mound the soil up around their emergent heads to blanch the new shoots. I will settle for the fluffy foliage of older ones through summer, excellent for cutting.

The next group of plants I select would make up the bulky backbone to my bed – the vegetables first.

Starting at the rear for height, I would plant a block of sweetcorn, selecting the seed of a hardy variety growing about 1.25 m/4 ft high called 'Polar Vee'. You plant sweetcorn in blocks rather than rows as it is wind pollinated. The first seed would need to be sown in gentle heat in April, hardened off in a cold frame avoiding the danger of late frost, and planted out in May or June.

I would also include the odd tomato plant in my border, selecting a tough small fruiting variety like 'Sub-Arctic Plenty', which needs no pruning or staking, and which my catalogue tells me 'has done very well from outdoor sowings when the seedlings have continually withstood several degrees of frost'. These little tomatoes would look good adjacent to my blue beans.

Next to the great leaves of my globe artichoke, how about some aubergines? Of course, my dream garden has a dream climate as well! But I could bring on some plants of the new 'Black Enorma' variety in pots and plant them out when it is warm enough. Being more realistic, however, why not some deep purple pickling cabbage – the variety called 'Red Drumhead', which should be sown

in spring for autumn and early winter harvesting – and next to this (for foliage contrasts again) some roots of Florence fennel or finocchio, having the added advantage of good feathery foliage as well. Sow the seeds under glass and plant out in May. Earth over the swelling bulblets to blanch them, and water copiously to make them swell. Harvest in late summer and eat with a cheese sauce.

I need some flower colour in my border now, and I look at my list of daisy types. A very coarse daisy flower, and one of the easiest to grow, must be the sunflower, and I would sow a mass of these at the back of my border between the globe artichokes and the sweetcorn. Listed under helianthus, I would go for the variety growing only 1.25 m/4 ft high or so called 'Sunburst Mixed', which has a lovely range of colour from lemon through gold to bronze and crimson. Sow wherever you wish them to grow.

At the far end of the rear of my border I can combine the yellow daisy flower head with the useful tuber of the Jerusalem artichoke, 'Dwarf Sunray'.

For early spring colour flowering just after the daffodils, plant leopard's bane (*Doronicum orientale* or *D.* 'Finesse'), which is excellent for cutting. Adjacent to the doronicums, as they are over so early, I plan a mass of the good old perennial single white asters, or for added colour a favourite late summer blooming variety, *Aster × frikartii* 'Monch'.

Nearby, across my asparagus clump, how about some rudbeckia – the variety called 'Marmalade' sounds appetizing – large golden flowers with a contrasting black central cone.

For foreground colour and good grey foliage I have a mass of *Rhodanthemum hosmariense* – one of the freshest of daisies.

Then another favourite little blue annual daisy, the kingfisher daisy, is felicia, which I would plant at the front of the border, though pot marigolds would be nice too, and possibly more suitable.

I have forgotten my favourite burgundy-coloured gaillardia, with wine red

Many species of perennials are 'daisy' shaped and would work well in the fantasy border, especially helianthus, left, and blue *Aster × frikartii* 'Mönch' shown on the right with kniphofia and sedum.

flowers in late September; they would look good near my tomatoes. Once you get the daisy bug you can go on forever!

But back to the low growing vegetable masses. Slap in the middle of my planting I must have some spectacular Swiss chard 'Rainbow' with brilliant orange and yellow stems in late summer until frost. This can be sown in the ground after frost in spring.

And on the other side of my seakale I would plant a massive beetroot behind the white daisies. Their purple foliage would look good, and if I see the variety 'Burpee's Golden Globe', I can boil the foliage tops as well as eat the golfball-sized beets.

Near the beets (which come in late summer) I would grow for earlier interest a group of curious tree onions which form bulblets at the top of their fleshy stems, and which can be pickled or use chopped in salad. They are known as the Egyptian tree onion.

The odd lettuce would be useful in my border, too. They look so crisp and crunchy – I would select the variety 'Tom Thumb', which has a good rosette head, and would be very tempted by mouth-watering 'Buttercrunch'. These two would be sown *in situ*.

The fantasy veg border includes the basics plus a little something for the bees and the eyes. Adding plants that attract pollinators to a garden, like alliums or bee balm, can be beneficial. Investigate companion planting to help reduce pests as well.

To balance my tree onions at the other end of the foreground border I would plant some leeks, not giant ones, but a few of the variety 'Musselburgh Improved'. These would make a good visual mass at the end of the border through the year from when they are sown until they are picked in winter, but a block of garlic (*Allium sativum*) would look just as good.

Finally, I must have a mass of ornamental flowering cabbage or kale in the middle of my group for autumn and winter pleasure. There are many to choose from, and the range of colours moves from creamy white to patterning of pink, carmine and purple. These would look delicious in front of the orange stems of chard.

And odd front spaces might be filled in with sowings of French parsley for its lovely foliage.

There it is – my dream border – selecting, grouping and picking its produce make so much more appetizing dreams than counting sheep!

## HERBS

Heat, salad and herbs seem to run together. Don't you long for the earliest tomatoes dressed with olive oil and basil, mint with your new potatoes, and a cold sorrel soup?

Which brings me to a consideration of herbs in general, for spring is the time to plant so you have them in time to fulfil your summer fantasies, or at least some of them!

And the joy of herbs is that they are so easy to grow. They like a poor soil in the main, though you should lighten a clay one with coarse sand or fine grit to open it up. Herbs like heat and in the main full sun. Mint and chives are the exception, for they will stand some shade.

Having none of the vigour of herbs grown in open ground, the less rampant ones may also be grown in window boxes though they will need regular feeding. I love the idea of circular hanging baskets of curly leafed parsley.

The herbs you grow depend on your site and what you want them for. If it's for the occasional snip for cooking, you might well use these very decorative plants among perennials for bulk. Fluffy fennel, purple and green, look wonderful with nigella (love-in-a-mist) or delphiniums, for instance. Rosemary complements shrub roses, while grey sage can edge a border and variegated lemon balm enlivens a yellow planting, with perhaps some golden feverfew

Herbs look wonderful in relaxed mixed borders, not just herb gardens. Herbs can also help with pest control in flower gardens. For example, alliums (in the onion family) deter aphids, so they are good companion plants for roses.

Some herbs are evergreen in many climates, like sage and thyme, while others must be planted annually like dill and basil. Some can be grown in pots and can be brought inside during the coldest months but may struggle if the air in your home is too dry.

mixed through. Thymes you can grow through your paving stones, though it's the taller shrubby ones that are used in bouquet garni (with tarragon, parsley and bay). Bay makes quite a large shrub, so site it carefully.

For more serious herbal cooking, you will need larger areas of herbs, which could be grown in blocks in the vegetable garden perhaps, or even as a patterned chequerboard with slabs between for easier access. You will need masses of chives, parsley – the curly leaved and larger leafed French or Italian (I think the latter has more flavour), French tarragon, dill and the various basils, including the large and small leafed green, and the decorative purple form called 'Dark Opal'. You need lots of sorrel to make a soup, for like spinach it goes to nothing when cooked. And have you ever thought about growing your own garlic and having a store of it for winter? Of chervil you need only a little; its strong celery flavour is dominating if overused. Of marjoram, too, you need only one or two plants.

I use lots of mints, their various flavours being wonderful with lettuce in salad or mixed with lemon balm for a summer Pimm's. I particularly like eau de Cologne mint, though the best culinary one is probably Bowles's mint, which grows up to 0.5–1 m/20–39 inches in height. Mints are invasive and rampant (making a good deciduous ground cover) and need to be restrained. Grow them separately in tubs or pots.

While herbs do flower, of course, they also have very fine foliage, and used decoratively can be a major part of the herbaceous border, though they are equally decorative allowed to ramble on their own. Unless you have unlimited time be wary of trying a mediaeval knot layout of herbs – which is so often recommended – for herbs are rampant. They self-seed and need dividing every so often, and to coax them into decorative shapes is asking for hours of work. You could add colour to your herb garden by including nasturtiums and pot marigolds, both useful in salads.

These are only a few basic culinary herbs; there are many more for cosmetic use, for medicinal use, for encouraging bees and butterflies, for dyeing and so on.

## NARCISSUS

Start thinking about next year's spring bulbs right in springtime; do not leave it until autumn, when all too often by the time you have sent off your order or got to the garden centre the best varieties have gone. Further, by thinking of your order now you can see exactly where you have the gaps which need filling, instead of guesswork later for, of course, once the foliage has died down you can't remember what was where!

As tedious as it might now appear, I would suggest drawing up a plan for yourself, so that you can mark quite clearly where the gaps are. You might also note which clumps need lifting and thinning so that your groupings appear more natural. It is all too easy to take up rectangular turfs when planting the bulbs, and popping in twenty or so, and the result is a tight little group. Multiply this technique and you can create a sort of staccato of blobs of colours, very far from the look which nature intended. And little rings of colour at the base of apple trees always seem a bit tacky.

I would suggest that you consider a shape of bulb planting within your overall layout where the grass is allowed to remain longer until all the bulb foliage

Narcissus look lovely both in lawns and in informal borders but remember to let their foliage die back completely before removing.

Tulips are a better choice in formal plantings but they often die back after a couple of years. You can easily manage this problem if you grow spare tulips in pots in autumn and plant them in spots where they are needed the following spring. This is easier than trying to remember where to plant in the autumn but you will have to protect them from mice and other rodents.

within the mass has died down. This way you are spared the yellowing tufts of foliage of individual groupings within your lawn and you might even get an early crop of wildflowers in the grass before all are cut in summer. Of course, if you select only early varieties of narcissus, you can mow your grass earlier. The earlier the flower head, the smaller it is usually, but this is a virtue on an exposed site since they are not so likely to be broken in the wind.

Narcissus varieties have a natural look which I believe is better growing in grass, or even coming through gravel, than planted in beds. For this more formal situation I would consider planting hyacinths or one of the many types of tulip.

To see the great range of narcissus and daffodils available, I would suggest a visit to a local spring flower show if there is one near you.

A wild type of narcissus is *Narcissus bulbocodium* (above centre), which is known as a species narcissus. The hybridized forms of the species tend to be much easier to grow and are more robust. The varieties of these hybridized forms are at the smaller end of the daffodil scale and are ideal for naturalizing in grass. They include 'February Gold', 'February Silver', 'Peeping Tom', 'Beryl' and the poeticus varieties (above left).

You may also grow the wild daffodil of northern Europe – the Lent lily, called *N. pseudonarcissus*, which grows to 15 cm/6 inches in height. A larger form double that size is *N. pseudonarcissus* subsp. *gayi*.

## CLIMBERS

It's pleasant to walk round your garden in the evening in springtime, tucking in the advancing shoots of early climbers, and seeing whether others are emerging.

It's also the time to check on the supports for those climbers, for after a while it often seems that the climber is holding the trellis and their original roles have become reversed.

We use the word climber, in fact, to describe all sorts of plants which can grow either on or against a wall. In the US they are all vines, an equally misleading term. So before deciding on the right support you need to know the modus operandi of the plant.

Many wall subjects are just tender shrubs, which get greater protection by being grown against a wall, and into this category go the early almond scented, yellow flowering *Azara microphylla*, some of the fancy buddleias like *Buddleja colvillei*, many ceanothus, the yellow flowering *Fremontodendron californicum*, some hebes, lemon verbena and even (in a small town garden) camellias, though the wall should not face east in that case.

California flannel bush (*Fremontodendron californicum*) can be trained to grow up a wall with a little support.

These woody wall shrubs only need holding back to the wall with a tie, and any shoots growing forward should be removed.

Real designated climbers will need greater support, though some of the favourite climbing roses simply need tying back to the wall. Many others are quite vigorous, however, such as *Rosa* 'Mermaid', so you will need a ladder to manage them since they get up to the first floor very quickly.

The type of support which I prefer for climbers is that given by plastic coated wires stretched taut between masonry nails in the wall. All can be bought at a garden centre or hardware shop. The wires are more or less flush with the wall and are used to tuck new shoots behind.

Ideally your wire supports should entirely cover your wall, fence or house elevation. Make a squared pattern to work with your doors and windows, either to the dimensions of window bars or some other architectural feature. They need not be more than a 30 or 45 cm/12 or 18 inches square.

Winter flowering shrubs like quince need less support as they get older but benefit from regular pruning to keep their shape. Check to be sure you prune at the right time for all shrubs so you don't accidentally cut off the next season's flowers.

I avoid trellis work as it is expensive and stands out as a feature, when in fact you want the plant upon it to be the eyecatcher. Unless well made and maintained, wooden trellises can also rot quite quickly.

Another method of supporting wires about 5 cm/2 inches away from the wall is to set vine eyes into the wall as the support. These are made of metal and are useful to incorporate into an older brick or stone wall where they can be driven in more deeply. The wires run horizontally and, being further out from the wall, are useful to push woodier material such as morello cherry stems or a large vine behind.

Quick growing climbers which will support themselves once you have directed them might include the golden hop (*Humulus lupulus* 'Aureus'), the passion flower (*Passiflora caerulea*), *Eccremocarpus scaber* and Russian vine (*Fallopia baldschuanica*), in addition to forms of clematis.

Annual climbers from seed such as nasturtium, canary creeper, *Cobea scandens* and morning glory can be trained up and through the same sort of wires.

Rambling roses, and things like honeysuckle and *Solanum jasminoides*, will also grow through the same type of support – though many vigorous ramblers will grow successfully through a host plant as well.

Another type of climbing plant is the twiner, and into this category go sweet peas and runner beans, though these only produce annual growth.

Ivies and climbing hydrangea ultimately need no support since they cling to the wall themselves, though both need a helping hand to start them off.

When planting any form of wall plant, do not set it too close to the wall where the soil dries out – a common fault. Position at least 45 cm/18 inches from the wall and train the plant back towards it.

Roses and other climbers can be trained to grow up trees and shrubs as well as walls and pergolas.

## COVER IT UP

At this time of year, late spring, there are an awful lot of weeds about, and the term 'ground cover' keeps coming up as though this were the magic solution to keeping them at bay. In some cases it can be, but let's look at the problem before exploring the solution.

In creating a garden, of course, you are trying to push back what would grow naturally – nature abhors open ground – and to introduce alien, cultured plants to the site. When the natives show themselves, we complain. You could make life considerably easier for yourself by going 'green' at this stage and seeing these intruders as essential 'natives' within your own microclimate!

The object of planting ground cover is to stifle the weeds – but these are only annual weeds in the main, and no plant will control the really invasive perennial ones; the cowboys such as buttercups, silverweed, ground elder and couch grass still need restraining. So before contemplating a mass planting of ground coverers, it is essential to clear your soil really thoroughly by removing all weed roots, since the combination of weed through ground cover is seldom appealing!

For maximum effect, a ground-cover planting should be evergreen, though some deciduous shrubs with branches to the ground will have the same effect.

Hydrangea 'Annabel' is effective as a ground cover and unlike many hydrangeas can be cut back in spring because it blooms on new wood.

The berberis family (both deciduous and evergreen) are low growers, as is choisya, which is evergreen. Then all forms of cornus are good, the brooms (cytisus), elaeagnus and escallonia. Hydrangeas are excellent, along with Portuguese laurel, pyracantha (grown as a shrub), rhododendron, ribes and rosemary.

Then there are the low growing and ground-covering roses – of which I suppose 'Nozomi' is the best known with its pearl pink flowers, but there are others available, too. Some of the smaller shrub roses, like *Rosa rugosa* 'Max Graf', will spread by rooting outwards, and *R. r.* 'Fru Dagmar Hastrup' has single pink flowers and large crimson autumnal hips. Incidentally, you can grow ramblers along the ground as a summer ground cover by pinning the shoots down as they grow.

For many, the ground-cover plant they need is one that both smothers weeds and grows in a dry shaded place as well. For these conditions I would suggest low growing cotoneasters like *Cotoneaster dammeri*, and the more vigorous *C.* 'Hybridus Pendulus', which can get to about 2.5 m/8 ft across. Also epimediums have creeping roots which put up fine evergreen glossy leaves and delicate flower sprays in spring. The vigorous spreader *Euphorbia robbiae* is also excellent with its yellow/green flower heads about 45 cm/18 inches high and evergreen rosettes of green foliage.

The cranesbill geraniums are excellent; my favourite is *Geranium* 'Rozanne', having bright blue flowers throughout summer, and it looks lovely in cool shade.

Most of the ivies make excellent ground cover, though watch that they do not go up into trees. Hypericum is an old yellow-flowering favourite, making a very good mat to smother anything. Lamium, which comes in various coloured

Rugosa roses (left) and epimediums (right) are very different in habit but both perform well as ground cover in the right setting.

leaf forms, is good but can become rampant as it roots as it goes along. It needs a good cut back from time to time.

In the United States liriope is used a lot and is a useful plant since its grape-hyacinth-like blue flowers come late in summer. It grows as a clump so you need plenty of them.

Then there are quite a range of mahonias which grow well, even in the poorest soils. The ground covers are excellent, as are forms of *Mahonia aquifolium*, which spread by underground suckers.

Pachysandra, or Japanese spurge, can be either dark green or variegated and creates a sort of carpet with greenish flowers early in the year. There is also a fine-leafed low-growing form of laurel, *Prunus laurocerasus* 'Zabeliana', which makes a good shrubby cover for larger spaces, while a shrubby suckerer is sweet box or *Sarcococca humilis*, which flowers in late winter and has an exquisite scent.

I'm very fond of *Tiarella cordifolia* or foam flower, for it has delicate heart shaped leaves and spires of fluffy white flowers. And a good old standby is periwinkle or vinca. I prefer *Vinca minor* ('Bowles's Variety' has violet-blue flowers), which is not so vigorous as *V. major*.

Do not be afraid of buying a number of each type of ground cover to create a good solid mass. Most grow fast and can be depended upon to eventually hold a bank liable to subsidence as well. In such a situation, you might plant through coarse chicken wire pegged down to maintain the level.

Pachysandra (left) has a wonderful fragrance and is evergreen while the more ephemeral tiarella (right) dies back in winter.

## SOME ROSEY THOUGHTS

Roses are not a particular passion of mine, which doesn't mean I don't like them either. Like 'horses for courses', there are 'roses for places'. My own garden isn't one of them as I live on gravel overlying chalk – both of which roses hate.

If I really push myself to analyse what I think of roses – it goes something like this.

I find embarrassing the whole 'Roses of Olde Englande' syndrome, and the traditional formal rose garden of endless geometry is something of a bore. Further, for approximately four or five months of the year in winter, I do not like the twiggy look of roses if they are not underplanted. Now if one has a large enough garden the space especially for roses can be separate, but for the average smaller garden, a hole cut out of a lawn for two dozen mixed Hybrid Teas is not a pretty sight in winter – or summer actually. Individual cut roses in a bowl look wonderful and smell even better, but for this purpose I can grow the roses lined up in a cutting garden just as well.

The vogue for formal garden layouts where geometrical shaped beds are edged with box and/or lavender and are then infilled with white 'Iceberg' Floribunda roses is rather pretty except that it has become a cliché, and one groans at seeing yet another permutation on the same theme.

Anything with white flowers is considered rather chic. 'It's so cool, my dear,' they say. That's all we need in the heat of summer!

Having got that out of my system, what I do like very much are old-fashioned shrub roses which you probably know as David Austin roses. Actually, he is only one of a number of shrub rose growers, but he seems to have managed to export both his roses and his name very successfully.

One of the disadvantages of the old roses is their comparatively short flowering period, but there are strains which perform for an extended period. Foliage colours vary quite a lot with this group, and some have a fragrance. Many also have splendid autumnal colours and fruits or hips. (I am purposely not giving variety names as I do not know whether you have the same roses in your country.)

Shrub roses mix very well with a general planting of shrubs, and the graceful form of

Rose hips add so much interest to the garden in autumn and come in a variety of shapes, sizes and colours.

some makes them ideal for naturalizing in rough grass to create a wild effect. Shrub roses could, I think, be very well associated with wild perennial masses too, and with some kinds of grasses.

Increasingly, I am interested in the class of rose known as the ground-cover rose. They are not unlike small ramblers and can serve the same very useful function as a low growing juniper, for instance.

You can, of course, pin down a rambler rose with wire to grow either up or down a bank or to be a sort of ground cover as well. I love rambler roses on a wall, and well-pruned climbers, too. I say 'well-pruned' as one wants to see flowers all over the plant, not just along the top.

Recently, following the vogue for the romantic Jekyll-type garden, roses are being grown through host trees, and while the idea is nice, in reality I now think I find it all a bit of a mess. I've tried it in my own garden, and I have to edit both the tree and the rose so much to make them mutually attractive that it isn't really worth it.

I am nothing if not perverse – let me finish by saying that there is nothing quite like the sharp sweet fragrance of roses on a June morning. It's the very essence of an English country garden. At one time I lived in Iran, where there are fields of roses grown for the manufacture of rose water – and I could never reconcile that smell with the Middle East. I would probably be just as difficult about it in other regions, but then you don't have to take on all my hang-ups, do you?

The fragrance of roses on a June morning epitomizes an English country garden.

## SHRUB ROSES

Late each spring I try to get to grips with the wide selection of shrub roses, and by the end of June I have quite a few names at my fingertips and I recognize the flowers that go with them. But come the next June I know that I will have forgotten what goes with what, and I start again. In order to help me remember the many types, I'm now categorizing old roses and hopefully a little historical association will fix them in my mind.

Species roses are the pure roses of nature, and in the catalogues are prefixed by 'Rosa'. Of this group I know *R. damascene versicolor,* the damask rose of York and Lancaster, a striped red and pink job; *R. eglanteria* is the common sweet briar, whose foliage smells deliciously of apples. The little single Austrian yellow rose, *R. foetida,* is not dissimilar (though its flower is paler) to *R. hugonis,* though it has ferny foliage. *R. moyesii* is a favourite, having single, blood red flowers, with the added attraction of splendid flagon shaped hips of waxy red in autumn. The twelfth-century *R. mundi* is a handsome old rose with splashes of pink and white on a crimson background. *R. primula* – the incense rose – is one of the earliest bloomers; though its scent is lovely, it's a little 'thin' as a plant. *R. glauca* 'Rubrifolia' self-seeds all over my garden and I love its plum-grey foliage and bright orange hips, but its single pink flowers are not really an asset.

Both *R. moyesii* and *R. glauca* have sensational rose hips in autumn which birds love.

After the species roses come the Centifolia group of cabbage roses, whose coarse, lax growth can often be quite prickly. This form is partly derived from Alba type roses. The most famous in the cabbage group are the Gallicas, like 'Cardinal de Richelieu', a velvety maroon gallica rose with a good scent. I love it. And the old cabbage Provence rose, *R. × centifolia*, has great pink, globular blooms of scent. 'Chapeau de Napoléon' is an interesting crested pink moss rose with a frill of green round its bud, while 'Fantin Latour' is another old favourite, having a flattened, full-petalled blush pink flower on a good bush. 'Félicité Parmentier' I would like to know and haven't yet found, with pale yellow buds opening to a neat blush rosette – she's scented too. 'Hebe's Lip' is a damask rose I can't resist, red in bud though later creamy with a reddish tint.

'Madame Hardy' is a good white among the old varieties, with cupped flowers and dark green leaves. 'Maiden's Blush' is an old Alba rose, having blush pink flowers and beautiful blue-grey foliage. The flowers have a strong sweet scent. 'Nuits de Young' has the darkest maroon flowers of all moss roses, with yellow stamens intensifying their rich velvety texture.

'Tour de Malakoff' has a good relaxed growth; large paeony-like magenta flowers, flushed purple but fading to lilac-grey, make it an exceptional old rose, too.

Another favourite old moss is 'William Lobb'. The large clusters of blooms vary from deep crimson purple to lavender. All these old roses are wonderful planted with lavender, cistus, purple sage and rosemary.

R. 'Cardinal de Richelieu' is wonderfully fragrant.

A later nineteenth-century group of roses are the Bourbons, popular in Victorian times for their repeat flowering characteristics, and having in the main French nomenclature. The roses I know in this group include 'Mme Isaac Pereire', with large, deeply scented crimson-purple blooms; 'Mme Pierre Oger', with charming tight little cabbage flowers of a pale silvery pink; 'Louise Odier', with camellia-type flowers of rose pink; and, last but not least, 'La Reine Victoria', who in fact sported both 'Mme Pierre Oger' and 'Louise Odier'. She is pink, rather upright in growth with a marvellous fragrance.

Of the Macrantha group, not dissimilar to a Bourbon rose, a great favourite is R. 'Raubritter', which trails as well. It has cupped, clear pink flowers with a fragrance.

The roses which were hybridized in the twentieth century are either Hybrid Musk roses, whose flowers are borne in large clusters, or the

modern shrub roses, which might well have a mixed progeny. Their colours are stronger, and they have the quality of repeat flowering too.

'Buff Beauty', which I love, is a Hybrid Musk; its form is relaxed and its flowers are warm apricot-yellow with a scent. 'Cornelia', too, comes into this category. She is coppery pink, keeps flowering on and on, and is therefore excellent for cutting. 'Felicia' is another Hybrid Musk that makes a good shrub, with two-tone flowers of clear silvery salmon-pink. And then 'Penelope' has grey foliage and soft creamy pink flowers.

Of the moderns, 'Fritz Nobis' I know, pink again but with a delicious clove scent, and 'Maigold', though it makes just as good a climbing rose – it's a gorgeous deep yellow with a scent. Finally, 'Nevada' makes a superb shrub with great arching branches literally smothered with cream-coloured single blooms both at this time of year and then again in August – it is spectacular!

Inevitably, synonymous with the word 'rose' comes the word 'disease' but shrub roses are tough in the main. An interesting fact seems to be that the more you water your roses overhead the less disease of any sort you get, but don't let the fear of disease put you off trying some of these superb plants in the garden. Check out your types, though, since photographs do them little justice. You need to see the overall plant shape, the foliage and flower texture, and most of all smell the fragrance.

In London I find the rose garden in Regent's Park one of the very best places to get to know the old rose varieties. Find your local rose garden and take a good look around to see what you like best.

Both 'Mme Pierre Oger' and 'Buff Beauty' thrive at Denmans. Not all roses bloom repeatedly throughout summer so if this is important to your garden scheme be sure to research those which do. It is also important to prune roses at the end of winter but some roses, like the ramblers, must be pruned in summer after they bloom instead.

## HOLLY

If you have an ordinary holly in your garden, December is probably about the only time of year when you take much notice of it, for it will be hung with berries and you then have the pleasure of cutting sprigs with which to decorate the house.

The word holly or holm is from Old English *holen* or *holegn*, which was itself derived from the Latin word *ulex* – actually the generic name for gorse – but it was confused in the Middle Ages with the word *ilex* – the Latin name for holly!

Since Roman times holly has been used as an emblem of goodwill during the festival of Saturn, celebrated on 17, 18 and 19 December, and this significance has probably moved through into Christian custom for the decoration of both home and church.

Our common native holly – *Ilex aquifolium* (*aqui* means prickly) – is probably the plant considered in legend, also being an evergreen, as a symbol of eternal life. It is this quality which makes it such an asset in the garden in winter, whether either free shaped as a specimen or used as a hedging plant. For even in town it is tough, withstanding both a polluted atmosphere and the worst exposure.

Holly berries are eaten by birds but often not until late winter.

The holly family is enormous, over 400 cultivars being listed, with forms in all sizes, with both prickly and smooth leaves, and with silver as well as gold variegations in the foliage available. So, it is a hardy, handsome, permanent addition to any garden, indifferent to sun or shade, and growing pretty well in most conditions.

In medieval times holly was said to possess special healing powers, and a lost traveller would always look for a holly bush under which to shelter and be safe from evil spirits. I do hope that you will not have to resort to this, but if you do, be sure to pick a form with spineless leaves.

## DECK YOUR HALLS

At the close of the year when our cultivated harvest is gathered in, nature's harvest of berries comes into its own. When the leaves go, late in autumn, they really stand out and provide some of the few spots of colour in the short, dull days of winter. They not only brighten up the garden and hedgerows but provide stable food for birds and small rodents. A heavy crop of berries is said to forewarn us of a hard winter. I do not think that this can be scientifically proven, and, ominously, if you believe in old wives' tales, there is a lot of it about this year!

The catalogues would suggest that birds will not eat cotoneaster berries, which are some of the brightest, though they make a meal of the heavy clusters overhanging my car of *Cotoneaster lacteus*, which is evergreen too. I regularly curse both the birds and the berries at this time of year and do nothing about it! Nearby we have a smaller cotoneaster – C. 'Rothschildianus', which is hung with yellow berries borne singly along the twigs. This is a striking and unusual shrub. There are many more in this huge family, which will grow well in both clay and chalky soil.

I think most people are aware of the 'firethorns' – the pyracanthas, which are close relatives of cotoneasters. This is another easy evergreen family surviving in shade or half-shade as well as sun. They all flower profusely – white in June – and are ablaze at this time of year with yellow, orange or red berries. Steer clear of the older form of *Pyracantha coccinea* 'Lalandei', which is subject to scab and fireblight disease. Pyracanthas can be grown on a wall, pruned as a hedge or used as a good infill shrub.

Cotoneaster (left) and pyracantha (right) are good infill shrubs that provide structure and winter interest.

There are not many occasions when I would extol the virtues of privet – it's such a greedy shrub. But next time you are out for a drive on the Downs, see it growing in pure chalk, even under the drip of trees and covered this time of year with small black berries, loved by birds and game. This is common privet, *Ligustrum vulgare*. While other privets will flower and berry if they are left unclipped, the fruit crop is not nearly as heavy as the wild form.

Another good semi-wild shrub with winter interest is the snowberry (partridge berry as it is called in the USA for obvious reasons). Symphoricarpus will grow anywhere in the worst places. Some forms sucker vigorously to create a matt of vegetation; all are heavy with white or pink berries at this time of year. Of the non-suckering type, *S.* × *doorenbosii* 'Magic Berry' has masses of carmine fruit, while 'Mother of Pearl' has large round berries that are white-tinted pink. There is an excellent planting of these for about a half mile on the approach to Terminal 4 at Heathrow, I noticed the other day.

At the other end of the spectrum of shrub sophistication, I would list *Pernettya mucronata* – it's ericaceous, however, and prefers a lime-free soil. You see it in many garden centres locally (not marked as liking an acid soil), and at this time of year its red, crimson, pink or white berries stand out. To make it bloom, however, a male plant is needed to every three female ones.

All my berrying plants have been shrubs – but a marvellous perennial for this time of year is the evergreen *Iris foetidissima*. Having small ochre yellow flowers marked with brown in June, it really comes into its own now with huge pods of orange seeds which hang well into the New Year. This iris will stand dry shade and even grows in pure chalk.

But for the joy of both its glossy foliage – sometimes green and sometimes variegated – and its gleaming masses of red berries at this time of year, as the carol reminds us, 'the holly bears the crown.' Our native holly, *Ilex aquifolium*, is common as a prickly hedgerow plant; the wood is very hard, and is the lightest in colour of our native timbers. But for Christmas decoration, and incidentally as an extremely tough shelter shrub, try some of the garden varieties. Holly has the added advantage of growing well in shade – though it will be slower – and it will thrive in almost any well-drained soil. It will also stand exposure to the sea. I prefer the more pyramidal growing hollies, the type whose leaves are not prickly.

A good green variety with regular crops of red berries is *I. a.* 'J. C. van Tol'. A variety with gold-edged foliage and red berries is *I.* × *altaclerensis* 'Golden King', while *I. a.* 'Argentea Marginata' has broad leaves with silver margins.

Perhaps the best yellow-berried form of holly with bright green leaves is *I. a.* 'Pyramidalis Fructu Luteo'. (How's your Latin bearing up?) There are many, many more hollies. Check them out in your Hillier catalogue if you are interested.

Incidentally, when choosing holly with berries in mind, do not forget that they are generally single sex, so you will need to buy one plant of each sex to be sure of berries.

*Iris foetidissima* is one of two iris native to Britain. Its flower is delicate and not terribly showy but its berries, which are revealed when the seed capsule bursts in autumn, are fantastic.

Holly traditionally represented masculinity – the spikes I suppose – while ivy stood for femininity, and the combination of both at Christmas promised fertility to the household. It was essentially ivy leaves that were used in wreaths and garlands, but at this time of year you will find certain shrubby ivies covered with green seed heads, which also turn black later on.

The Christian Church adopted many of these early pagan traditions. In Scandinavian countries holly is known as Christ-thorn since the colour of its berries was said to symbolize Christ's blood and suffering.

Interestingly, a plant which the Church has never had anything to do with is mistletoe, for in Norse legend it was responsible for the death of Balder, the god of light (at the end of the year). Clusters of mistletoe (*Viscum album*) with their forked branches, pale yellow-green leaves and clear white berries can often be seen in wintertime perched on deciduous trees – poplar, lime and farmed in apple orchards too. Mistletoe is a true parasite for it derives its food entirely from the tree on which it grows, at no time coming into contact with soil. In previous times superstitious farmers would feed a piece of mistletoe to a cow which calved at New Year to ward off evil. While one might not go that far now, today's custom of kissing under mistletoe may be connected, for it was the earliest Scandinavian belief that if enemies met beneath it, they would forgive each other and embrace. Aah!

## USING BULBS

It seems that in late winter an odd assortment of containers accumulates, lurking about at the kitchen door. Their contents are inevitably the dying heads of bulbs which were forced for Christmas, some white narcissus, the odd amaryllis, and a long-spent cyclamen or two. Actually, only the narcissus made it on time, their spring scent filling the room before their heads flopped over in an expensive excess of yuletide heating. The amaryllis put on an obscene amount of growth and a noble red flower head for New Year. The cyclamen was a present, and it too suffered from internal exposure, becoming leggy and floppy until the flowers finally petered out. The plant is still alive (although disliking its external exposure now), for I carefully watered the plant only from the base by soaking it so that its corm did not rot from top watering.

Cyclamen is wonderful when it is blooming but needs a dormant period once it is finished. The leaves will eventually die back so stop watering and place in a cool place for two months before watering them again.

I cannot ever bring myself to throw these spent plants away and I must now get down to doing something about them. Gardening journals would have us plunge the pots (they love plunging) under the potting bench, allowing the foliage to die down naturally, but they fail to say what happens if you haven't such a bench, and when the garden, a balcony or only a windowsill have to do.

*Amarylis are much more dramatic when planted in threes or more.*

If it's the garden, I would plant out the narcissus, when there is no frost in the ground, about 20–23 cm/8–9 inches deep, breaking up the rooty mass so that next year in spring they do not reappear as a little blob of colour. Make them into a random grouping, and although they will scarcely be elegiac next year, you will gain a prettier effect.

If you haven't a garden, allow the bulbs to dry out slowly and their green leaves to die down naturally. You can then reuse their soil or compost and store the bulbs in a dry place until planting them again in autumn, or simply allow the bulbs to remain in their pot but dry. In late October you should then water and feed the bulbs with a little bonemeal to activate them.

I feel sorry for the poor old amaryllis on its own, for the pot it came in seems so small and out of scale when in flower. Make a note to yourself to try to plant more than one amaryllis bulb next year for a mass of them – three all the same colour look spectacular. Incidentally, bought loose in autumn, they are cheaper.

After the amaryllis flower dies, it should be protected from frost for the bulb is not hardy. Pot it on into a container a little larger than whence it came in a well-drained general compost and allow it to rest until about Christmas time when you start to water it gently. It should then flower the following February. It you haven't a garden, store the bulb on a north-facing windowsill or out on the balcony, although until the frost has gone protect the bulb as far as possible by wrapping its pot.

Place your cyclamen in a similar position, though remember about watering it only from the base when it is time. Position your plant in light shade for it does not need excessive sunlight when growing.

If you are feeling brave, you could cut your cyclamen corm into two as you pot it on, using a sharp knife. Both the cyclamen and the amaryllis are not hardy and cannot be planted out. There are also lovely cyclamen that are hardy outdoors, including *Cyclamen coum* (below), which grows beautifully at Denmans.

The thing to remember about bulbs is that after flowering they die down naturally, but during this process they are also preparing their flowers for next season after a period of summer drought, for many come from the mountainous regions of the Caucasus, Turkey or Persia. Autumn and winter rain slowly activates their growth for spring flowering. The process may be commercially artificially 'forced' for an early Christmas show, but on the home front it will revert to the natural and later cycle.

Whether your cyclamen is hardy or not, it will need a period of dormancy over the summer before it can bloom again.

# IF I COULD SAVE ONE PLANT

I have been asked if I could save one plant from my garden – what's going to happen to it, I wonder – what would it be? An old apple tree. Why? Because it would give me pleasure throughout the seasons.

In winter I would enjoy the black twigginess of its crown. I prefer not to prune hard so I can retain a certain cragginess of my half-standard tree. In spring I would get pleasure from shows of pinky white blossom – both on the tree and fallen around it. In summer I would appreciate the shade of its arching limbs, and by autumn I would have a fine crop of my favourite Egremont Russet apples. This is the best russet with an excellent flavour ripening during late October or early November. And further, it's a local variety from Sussex, and I'm all for local varieties where possible.

Egremont Russet apples, which were first recorded in the 1870s, are one of the great joys of autumn.

If I was really sneaky I could establish some mistletoe on my tree for Christmas – and run a pale coloured old-fashioned flowering rose up the trunk to hang down in early summer, something like 'Félicité Perpétue' or 'Wedding Day', and I would have its fragrance as well.

# PART V:
# THE LAST
# WORD

## MORE TO IT THAN FLOWERS?

I have been musing about how gardens have changed since I first started designing fifty years or so ago.

I now inhabit a strange world with one foot still in the professional world visiting flowers shows and future garden sites, but with the other in the local garden centre or nursery. The left foot still seems to have very little idea of what the right is doing.

But perhaps I'm getting the issues confused? I'm interested in garden design and layout, which of course involves the selection of plant material: much of the media is concerned solely with actual growing and with plant welfare or husbandry.

But one follows the other surely?

Within my lifetime the concept of a garden has moved along hugely. At one time a garden needed to be of a considerable size to even get a rating – now we consider the smallest area just as feasible both as a garden and (certainly in summer) as an additional room to the house.

When I started writing about rooms outside, I was considering the younger family and how to make the most of what you have got both visually and practically with, somewhere down the line, eventual resale in mind. Now I

John, the first independent designer to show a garden at the Chelsea Flower Show (1962), won a Flora Silver medal for his representation of a garden room outside of a fictional town house. Controversial for the time, it was the first time an exhibition garden was about the garden as a living space rather than a collection of plants.

believe the younger family probably has more pressing needs than constructing a garden, and it is an older generation which has the time and need for a pleasant setting.

I think that location too now defines a garden much more than it used to. There is the inner-city space, there is the suburban sprawl, and then there is the rural garden. Each location conjures up a different picture in the mind's eye. But it is the small garden which gets most attention. I suppose not only are there more of these, but they can also be built as exhibition pieces at shows. Travel has undoubtedly opened people's eyes to the potential of the smallest space.

On the designer side of me, I begin to see outside installations called conceptual gardens, which to the horticulturally attuned eye at first seem strange, and to this oldie seem all too often at odds with their location, though I realize that that is not entirely their point.

I do see, however, that land art can say something for the designer, since the materials he or she uses are 'of the site' – and I think that this is important, and very much to do with the trend today of gardens being 'of their place'.

I think that at last we have moved along from gardens of other cultures, which always seem alien to me though we can assimilate their philosophy. What relates a garden to its location and the structure it surrounds are the materials of which it is built and how they are used (and its design, of course!).

When I started, concrete was the great new material. Modernist houses were built of it (though they were pre-war), but one saw it used in continental and Californian gardens, and when used well concrete is still a great medium.

And then we moved to brick. An exhibition in the 1970s of the work of Edwin Lutyens and Gertrude Jekyll showed how sympathetic a material it could be when well laid – though it was thought a bit retrogressive at the time.

One of three exhibition gardens John did with the Inchbald School of Garden Design paid tribute to Gertrude Jekyll and Edwin Lutyens.

'For a quick fix cover the whole wretched thing with decking!' We had this for a number of years, and then, for city bankers and tycoons, rooftop gardens with stainless steel water features. These were a bit too hard and industrial for many, so they became rusted, and were used to great effect in various garden exhibitions. And so, fashions move on and change.

The selection of plant material is a much more explosive subject, for this is what interests the gardener most – or would it be correct to say the older gardener? It takes time to become familiar with the vast range of plants which we are able to grow in this country. The young – with a more acute eco sense – are questioning whether because we *can* grow this range of plant material it means that we *should*. We are beginning to look far more closely at our native grasses and wild flowers in particular, not enough yet at native trees and shrubs, I fear. Is this a new romanticism? It is often presented as such as part of an 'escape to the country', which I constantly read in my Sunday supplements.

I think that there is an increasing interest in a 'sense of place'. We get it in the current mode of regional cooking on TV, we read about conservation and vernacular architecture, and we are even holidaying at home to experience our own countryside. It would be nice if the garden could reflect these changes as well. To a degree differing soils do affect what will or will not grow, of course; this alters the traditional look of a landscape, its walls and fences, and the farming practised upon it.

LEFT Using what grows locally, in combination with native and non-native plants, you can connect your garden to the local landscape and maintain its sense of place.

RIGHT Andrew Duff's 2019 Chelsea exhibition garden featured a clever balance of British native plants, strong lines, water and a David Harber sculpture, creating a sustainable, tranquil sanctuary in an urban environment.

Ducks nest at Denmans each year since the pond has been rebuilt.

The garden designer and the gardener must be aware of these changes; we are part of this cycle, not superior to it. This underlying idea of relating garden to region is at odds with the grander traditional garden concept of imposing a design, and then judging the merit of the layout by the number of alien plants that can be grown in it.

Increasingly, we strive for the wilder approach using more native plant material with less manicured grass, fewer beds to be cultivated, and planting which encourages birds, bees and butterflies. Where garden maintenance was once necessary, it is being replaced by garden management – quite a different process.

Inevitably, the discussion of wildlife in a garden brings the story to rabbits and deer, but walk anywhere in the countryside and you will see that it is not bare. Native plants define the feel of the countryside, which we are enjoying more and more: are we just growing the wrong things in our gardens?

ABOVE John again broke ground when he designed the first kitchen garden for exhibition at the Chelsea Flower Show in 1975.

LEFT At Chelsea 2017 nurserywoman Sarah Raven designed the Anneke Rice Colour Cutting Garden, a small, informal cutting garden devoted to herbs and flowers, supported by natural materials.

TOP RIGHT Dan Pearson's 2004 Chelsea exhibition garden combined natural materials and naturalistic plantings with a strong, clear layout.

RIGHT Cleve West's 2016 Chelsea exhibition garden was inspired by and was reminiscent of the ancient oak woodland on Exmoor National Park.

We may never get the plant person or the nursery owner to buy into this view, and it is probably where the country gardener will split from the urban one. Each of necessity will have a different approach.

Wild flowers can bridge this gap along with herbs, and they are becoming increasingly popular, but they are seasonal, do not have the visual strength of trees and shrubs, and are not really suitable for the urban plot.

The latest flower show gardens and the future garden exhibits have begun to explore new possibilities for garden spaces. The trend seems to be organic again, using natural materials. Many of the gardens are quite sculptural and are at the other end of the spectrum to traditional forms of decorative horticulture.

Many are quite subtle in their concept: evoked by a landscape and its vernacular idioms, a story or an interest in wild form and texture alone.

There is something astir out there, which is different and exciting. Can you feel it?

# INDEX

Page numbers in *italics* refer to illustrations.

in site assessment 105; specimen 37; topsoil depth for 163
trellis 20, 188, 189
trends in gardens 43, 44, 52, 208–210
triangular garden *128*, 128–129
triangulation 104
tulips *37*, *187*
twiners 190
two-dimensional patterns 79, 114
two-dimensional scheme to three dimensions 49, 50, 103, 124, 168

## U

United States 42, 43, 75
urban garden SEE town garden
urban terrace 23, 66–67, *67*
use of gardens 35, 44, 46, *101*, 101–102; by families 44–45, 99, 101, 106, 208–209; for people, but furnished with plants 99, 101, *108*, 109; sunlight and 160; week-a-year garden 35

## V

vegetable(s), in border with flowers 180–183
vegetable garden/patch 30, 45, *102*; in gardens of future 53
*Verbascum bombyciferum* (giant mullein) 166, 171, *178*, 179
vernacular, local 12, 31, 60, 70, 76, 90, 92, 130; observing and recording 94, *94*
vernacular architecture 43, 73, 157, 210
*Viburnum* (viburnum) 75, 143; *V. farreri* 168; *V. mariessii* 174–175; *V. tinus* 37, 168
views from garden *159*
views from house 21, 38, *38*, *51*, 63, 101, 109, 159; modern buildings 110–111; in site assessment 104; town garden 65
views into garden, limiting 160
*Vinca major* 193
*Vinca minor* 193
*Viscum album* (mistletoe) 202, 205
vistas, features at end of 24, *159*
*Vitis coignetiae* 177

## W

walls: colours in garden on 35, 65, 66; retaining 106, 107, 163; shrubs against 188–189

water 19, 136, 137–138, *139*; SEE ALSO ponds; pools of water; in built environment 138; in designs 136–138, *139*; in nature 137, 138, *139*; run-off 161–162; small scale and 137, 138; stainless steel water features 210
water plants 21
waterfalls *137*, *139*
watering, after planting trees/shrubs 173, *173*
waterlogging 154, 157
weeds 75, 93, 152, 158; annual 152, 158, 191; in compost 165; gravel gardening 171; ground cover to stifle 191, 192; perennial 152, 165, 191; removal 13, 191
week-a-year garden, creating 32–37, *33*, *34*
West, Cleve *213*
wild flowers 153, *153*, 154, *155*, 213
'wild' garden/wildness 25–26, 111, 211; reinterpretation 43
wildlife 53, 54, 153, 200, 211
wind 21; filtering 160; hedges/trees limiting 160; in town gardens 161
winter, garden tasks 32
winter interest, plants with 166–169, *167*, *189*, 200–201; berries, plants bearing 53, 199, *199*, *200*, 200–201; holly 199, *199*
wire supports 189
wisteria 177
wood 95, 96
woodland 21, 77, *77*, 151, 154

## Y

yew (*Taxus baccata*) 75
yucca 23

# ACKNOWLEDGEMENTS

## PUBLISHERS' ACKNOWLEDGEMENTS

The publishers have made every effort to contact holders of copyright works, whether text or illustrations. Any copyright holders we have been unable to reach are invited to contact the publishers so that a full acknowledgement may be given in subsequent editions.

For permission to publish the following articles (or earlier draft versions) the publishers would like to thank the following:

'What will be classed as the great gardens of the future?': *The Garden* magazine (Royal Horticultural Society), 1998

'A week a year garden': *Sunday Express*, 1987

'The genius of the place: thoughts on garden design': *House & Garden magazine, and Condé Nast which holds the copyright to this article, 1963*

'An introduction to Kazimir Malevich': *GallerySPD* magazine, 2013

'How I use water as a designer': written for *Gardens Illustrated* in 1993 for one of the magazine's very earliest issues

'Using sculpture in the garden': *The English Garden* magazine, 2003

'There's much to be learned from other people's gardens': *West Sussex Gazette*, 1992

'Winter interest at Denmans': *A Landscape Legacy*, Pimpernel Press, 2018

'Gravel gardening': *The English Garden* magazine, 2002

'Improving your lot': *The Evening Standard*, undated

'Planting trees and shrubs': *The Evening Standard,*1989

'Summer pruning': *The Evening Standard*, 1989

'Herbs': *The Evening Standard*, 1988 or 1989

'Narcissus': *The Evening Standard*, 1989

'Climbers': *The Evening Standard*, 1988 or 1989

'Cover it up': *The Evening Standard*, 1989

'Shrub roses': *The Evening Standard*, 1989

'Holly': *The Evening Standard*, 1989

'Deck your halls': *West Sussex Gazette*, 1992

'Using bulbs': *The Evening Standard*, 1989

'If I could save one plant': *Sunday Telegraph*, 2002

## PICTURE CREDITS

All illustrations © The John Brookes-Denmans Foundation, with the exception of the following:

© Andrew Duff: pages 6, 211 (below)

© Peter Gillespie: pages 18, 45 (below left)

© Elena Markitantova: page 87

© Nigel Philips: page 205

© Gwendolyn van Paasschen: pages 2, 4, 10–11, 15, 18 (above), 19, 24, 28, 29, 37, 40, 53, 74, 76, 77, 79, 84, 92, 94, 97, 98, 101, 102, 108, 110, 111 (right), 130 (above), 132 (above), 135, 139, 140, 143, 144–145, 146–147, 151, 152, 153, 156, 160, 162, 164, 165, 167, 168, 169, 170, 171, 173, 174, 175, 176, 177, 178, 180, 181, 182, 183, 184, 185, 186, 187, 188, 189, 190, 191, 192, 193, 194, 195, 196, 197, 198, 199, 200, 202, 203, 204, 206–207, 211 (above), 212 (below), 213

## AUTHOR'S ACKNOWLEDGEMENTS

The idea of publishing a selection of writings and lectures by John Brookes MBE first arose when I picked up a lever-arch file with the label 'Lectures 1990s' after John died. Not surprisingly, it was full of lectures he gave on design. They were varied, thorough, and in some cases, intensely thoughtful. In the subsequent process of developing an archive from the piles of John's unsorted papers, other articles, lectures, and drafts of equal interest emerged.

The fifty pieces included here, many of which were only in draft form, are timeless, just as many were ahead of their time.

This book is meant to reintroduce a new generation of gardeners and designers to the fundamental principles of garden and landscape design John introduced and is intended to provoke thought, raise questions, and kindle discussion about style, design, the environment, and what is appropriate.

This book would not have been possible without Ryan Adams, whose hard work starting the archive from scratch was essential. I would like to thank Elena Markitantova, and Noriko Hamamoto for providing material, insight and encouragement. Peter and Jean Richards, my beloved friends, offered essential non-gardener insight. Peter Gillespie, John's longtime friend and colleague, offered essential garden and design insight as he continues to do with respect to the restoration and maintenance of Denmans.

The book would not be a reality without the vision of the ever-brilliant team at Pimpernel Press, including Jo Christian, Gail Lynch, Becky Clarke, Emma O'Bryen, and the very patient Nancy Marten. Their insights have made the book better. It was an inter-lockdown visit with Jo and Gail that provided the impetus for making the book a reality. Thanks also to Louise Campbell for keeping me on track.

And thanks to Andrew Duff, John's dear friend and colleague, who provided the foreword and one of my favourite photos of John.

And to Alastair Shaw, whose advice was critical and well timed.

I am also deeply grateful to the team here at Denmans. They have endured more than my absentmindedness and middle-of-the-night emails. More importantly, they have thrown themselves headlong into the adventure and mission of restoring Denmans, John's home and garden of thirty-eight years.

On a personal note, I'd like to thank my friends for putting up with the long periods of distracted radio silence to which book projects inevitably lead. I'm especially and forever grateful to my daughter, Jane Makin, and her husband, Rahul Mehta, residents of Chicago, for their love and for their support for my life in England, which has seemed impossibly far away since March of 2020.

Last but absolutely not least, I'd like to thank my partner, Mike Palmer, for his endless (and I mean endless) patience, support, love, cups of tea, cappuccinos, and insights. Without him this book would have been infinitely more difficult to write, if not impossible, as without him it would be infinitely more difficult, if not impossible, to have restored Denmans.